Discovering
CHURCH FURNITURE

Christopher Howkins

© Shire Publications, 1969

Line drawings by the author

Shire Publications, Tring, Herts.

CONTENTS

SBN 85263075 1

INTRODUCTION

I love looking at churches, especially old ones, and the visitors' books show that many other people do too. "How old is it?" is a question I frequently hear, and to help with this question is one of the aims of this book. A few regional variations and local workshops are mentioned, but this aspect is too complicated for a book of this size, hence only brief historical notes. Obviously there have been some generalisations also.

Wherever possible I have used examples that I have seen myself. Next I used those kindly sent to me in response to requests. Otherwise I chose those pieces which are well documented, so that you can easily discover more yourselves. I have checked many of the examples but cannot guarantee they are still extant: I recorded one item and returned a few days later to sketch it, only to find that it had been stolen.

The drawings are my own. They are only sketches to give an impression of the piece, so are not to scale, and some have been simplified, especially in their surface decoration.

I hope the technical terms will not deter you: there are not so many as in cooking or gardening! (see the Bibliography for glossaries). 'Jacobean' is used in its broadest sense (very late sixteenth and early seventeenth century) unless the monarch is specified.

Furniture has to be functional, which adds another specification for the artist, thus frequently making the result a masterly work, but when also beautified in God's name, it can be superb. All churches have furniture, and there are over 16,000 parish churches alone, so there is an inexhaustible wealth to discover. I should be pleased to hear of your interesting discoveries, and will acknowledge all correspondence. Visiting churches is always rewarding: the bad has to be seen to appreciate the good, and churches can be visited summer or winter, wet or fine, country or city. I wish you all enjoyable days *Discovering Church Furniture*.

CHRISTOPHER HOWKINS

Haslemere, Surrey.

I should like to thank everyone who helped with this book, especially the publishers, the photographers, Mrs. M. L. Fox, Dr. R. H. Little, R. K. Lingard Guthrie, E. A. North, and K. J. Fryer.

ALTARS

Altars have been an essential part of the church since earliest times, and were originally wooden tables symbolising the Last Supper. At various times (e.g. 750 and 1076) they were condemned in favour of stone altars or *mensae*, but wooden ones have always persisted, though pre-Reformation ones are extremely rare.

Many mensae remain, a few in their original position. They can be from four to ten feet long, about three feet wide, and from four to twelve inches thick. The upper surface has a small consecration cross in each corner and one in the middle, to symbolise the five wounds of the Cross, although differing numbers are known. The Saxon mensa at **Corhampton**, Hampshire, has these crosses.

During the Reformation (c. 1550) most mensae were replaced by wooden tables. Many were used as paving stones, etc. The Norman one at **Wisborough Green**, Sussex, was found in the vicarage garden and restored to use. Many were destroyed, especially those with a cavity for relics, called a *confessio* or *sepulchrum altaris* which was concealed with a stone lid or *sigillum*. Queen Mary restored the mensae; Elizabeth in 1559 is said to have ordered the replacement of stone by wooden altars, but the wording of this injunction is not explicit, and many stone altars were tolerated.

However, there are many Elizabethan wooden **communion tables** left (**Blyford,** Suffolk). They have richly decorated bulbous ('melon') legs and ornamented rails, sometimes inscribed. Jacobean ones have less bulbous legs, not richly carved, but the rails are usually well decorated (**Dinton,** Buckinghamshire). Communion tables can be well seen where now redundant (**Warnford,** Hants.).

About 1550, side altars also went, but many have been restored in chapels. Former altars are indicated by piscinas in the walls (**Dunsfold,** Surrey).

There is a modern symbolic altar in the Crypt Chapel at **Bosham,** Sussex.

Reredoses

The reredos is the backing to the altar, which can range from Norman wall paintings in **St. Albans Cathedral** (oldest in the country) to the superb modern (1966) tapestry of John Piper's design in **Chichester Cathedral. Christchurch Priory,** Hampshire, has a Perpendicular stone screen or retable with niches and tabernacle work which, although not as good as some (e.g. **Winchester Cathedral**), does retain some of the original figures.

Durham Cathedral has the finest open tabernacle one. The wall behind is sometimes used: with niches (**Enstone**, Oxon.), with arcading (the finest is **Bristol Cathedral**) or a combination, of which the best is at **Somerton**, Oxon. Figure work is always religious, invariably the life of Christ, and most appropriate of all, the Last Supper. There are many Victorian marble examples of this. Far more attractive are the sculpted alabaster panels (**Drayton**, Berkshire) which were very popular in the fourteenth century. Painted wooden panels were also used: **Romsey Abbey**, Hampshire, has some very notable ones. Post-Reformation examples are rare outside **London**. The Wren churches have some fine ones, especially those of Grinling Gibbons (St. Mary Abchurch is magnificent). Many churches just have a curtain on three sides, which is the survival of the very early practice of surrounding the altar completely with curtains which were drawn together at the consecration in the Communion Service.

Roods had celures, and altars were likewise adorned, but remaining examples are extremely rare. **East Hendred**, Berkshire, and **Minster Lovell**, Oxon., are said to have decorated roofs above, whilst **Ludlow** and **Clun** in Shropshire have hanging testers.

Altar Rails

With the destruction of rood screens, it was necessary to find alternative protection for the altar from irreverent treatment by people and dogs. So in early Elizabethan days altar rails were introduced. Some are dated to prove that Archbishop Laud did *not* instigate them, only encourage them. There are many 'Laudian' rails remaining (**Langar**, Nottinghamshire) which are often as much as three feet high.

Mostly, altar rails stretch right across the chancel, but at **Altarnum**, Cornwall, right across the whole church. Occasionally they enclose three sides of the altar (**Ewhurst**, Surrey) and, very rarely nowadays, four sides (**Branscombe**, Devon). The wooden balusters usually have a central bulge, or can be treated like columns. Spiral ones are late seventeenth and early eighteenth century. In the eighteenth century wrought iron was used (St. Magnus-the-Martyr, **London**)—using the same principles as iron screens.

CHESTS OR COFFERS

Many churches today possess an old chest. Formerly all churches were compelled by law to have a chest and most churches had several: a few still have more than one. The Synod of Exeter, 1287, was one such occasion, but previous to that, in

1166, Henry II had ordered the same, to collect for the Crusaders. 'Saladin Tithe' was a land tax to help the cause in the Holy Land. It was collected in the churches, until it was amassed in Salisbury, all £6,000 of it. When parish registers were instigated in 1538, chests were once again required.

Chests were used for keeping money, relics, vestments, documents, registers, plate and other valuables. Oak was the primary timber used, for it was readily available, durable and, most important, very strong. However, there are several elm chests (**Eckington** and **Cleeve Prior** in Worcestershire and **Minster** in Kent) as well as chestnut and cedar, and cypress (**Cheveley,** Cambs.). Despite the post-Reformation enthusiasm for walnut, it was rarely used for church chests because it is too prone to worm attack.

The earliest chests to be found are Saxon (**Wimborne Minster,** Dorset) and from then onwards examples may be found until the Georgian period. After that they are rare, because chests had been superseded by chests of drawers, which, of course, were of little use in churches. During all this time there was considerable development in the art and skill required in their production, making it possible to classify them (see the following). Apart from their age, they are also interesting as examples of the work of the local carpenter and blacksmith who were employed to do the work. Very rarely was it of sufficient importance to require the services of more skilful craftsmen, although these chests are by no means unskilful. The rustic simplicity of the earliest chests is just as beautiful as the geometric carving that followed, or the elaborate figure and foliage carving of others.

Dug-out Chests

The dug-out chests, or monoxylons, are the earliest to be found. They date from Saxon times (**West Grinstead,** Sussex) to the thirteenth century, but the majority are twelfth century (**Marston Trussell,** Northants.) Probably Warwickshire has the most. Some dug-outs, it is suggested, are later than the thirteenth century, but this is most unlikely.

They can easily be identified because they have no joins (except the lid). They are, simply, squared-up tree trunks, hollowed out by hand with an adze. This was very laborious, especially as oak is such a hard wood, so the cavity is small. For example, the impressive Saxon dug-out in **Wimborne Minster,** Dorset, is 6½ feet long, but the cavity is only 22 inches long, 9 inches wide, and 6 inches deep. It is believed to have been used for keeping relics safe. Safe they were, for with no joints to prise apart, thieves would have to try and split open the solid log. The lid was rarely a weak point, as it was very thick and

Saxon dugout chest at Wimborne Minster, Dorset.

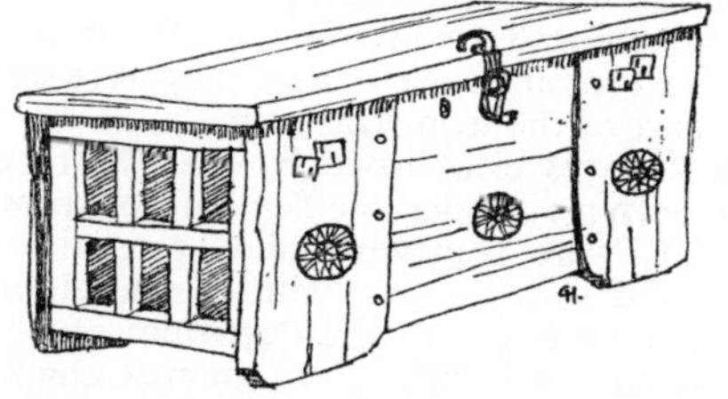

Thirteenth century chest at Stedham, Sussex.

had several clever iron locks (with different key holders, to reduce the risk of corruption).

Another safety precaution was to bind the chest round with numerous iron bands (**Bickenhill,** Warwicks.) to make breaking in even more difficult. This precaution persisted long after dugouts and is often very decorative, as at **Church Brampton,** Northants (a county with many good chests). Alternatively, or in addition to iron banding, some dug-outs were studded with large-headed wrought iron nails. **Hatfield,** Yorkshire, shows both these methods on the same chest. Iron is the only decoration of these chests; they were not touched by the carver but were, presumably, coloured.

Boarded Chests

A major development in chest making took place in the thirteenth century, namely joinery, resulting in the boarded or plank chests. These chests were made of large planks, with the back and the front nailed on to two ends with large wrought iron nails. The bottom was grooved and nailed in. The lid was also a plank, and still sometimes curved, and thus called a trunk.

This lid worked on a horizontal pivot like a hinge, which is most important. It can rarely be seen, especially as most chests are kept locked (presumably still in use). The pivot hinge lasted until the fifteenth century, but is largely superseded by strap hinges after the thirteenth century. With no iron hinges the joint was very vulnerable, and so to safeguard against breaking in, chains were stapled across the back, three of which remain at **Clymping**, Sussex.

These new designs were a great improvement, but there were many refinements to follow, although the principle was used thereafter. This new technique allowed much larger cavities, in deeper and wider chests, which thus did not need to be so long (some dug-outs are ten feet or more long). However, this crude joinery was often not strong enough to take the heavy contents, so ironwork is again used, to hold it all together and to restrict warping which also destroyed the shape. To aid this, iron feet were occasionally introduced to lift the wooden bottom clear of the damp floor. If strap hinges were used, they were sometimes extended to act as part of the iron strapping.

A guild of cofferers was established by the twelfth century, so there must have been a considerable demand for these chests. The mediaeval guilds were somewhat similar to the modern trade unions. They did not interfere with the development of church furniture, as they did with the development of printed illustrations. The guilds had their own chantry chapels with parclose screens and in most chantries there would be a chest for collecting money.

Stiled Chests

Towards the end of the thirteenth century a further development took place in the joinery of boarded chests. The front and back boards were tongued or tenoned into wide upright stiles or clamps, which extended below the bottom to form legs. These were necessary to keep the wood off the damp church floor. The ends were dovetail housed into the front and back, and further strengthened by a portcullis arrangement of thick battens. The lid, nearly always flat now, was still pivot hinged to begin with, but after the thirteenth century strap hinges were regularly used. Apart from these, ironwork was rarely used, except sometimes to reinforce the bottom. Locks and staples were numerous, sometimes ten or more.

During this period, **chip carving** was introduced, as roundels on the front. Some writers claim that chip carving is only found on chests. They are wrong. Chip carving was reintroduced on to Jacobean pulpits, but was shallower and more delicate, and not in roundels. However, long before these chests, the Norman masons were chipping out in stone the same roundels on fonts. These may be seen at **Reighton**, Yorkshire; **Bratton**, Devon; **Mevagissey** and **Launceston**, Cornwall. Similar designs were also cast into the lead font at **Long Wittenham**, Berkshire in the twelfth century. They were the work of the village carpenter and did not require the skill of a carver, as they only consisted of geometric patterns, simple in principle but elaborate in conception, as is soon discovered by those who try to sketch them. However, some respond to 'rubbing' like brasses, using thin strong paper and a pencil. These will be good enough to trace for a good copy. Always ask permission first. They were such as could be drawn with compasses and then chipped out. Typical chests of this description are at **Stoke D'Abernon,** Surrey and **Stedham,** Sussex.

Towards the end of the century chip carving developed beyond roundels and became arcading, following the same designs as the wooden screens and stone window tracery. In chip carving the sinkings are only scooped out, and were not properly sunk or moulded until the fourteenth century. A very fine example showing roundels and arcading is at **Clymping,** Sussex.

The fashions of screens, windows and tombs continued in the development of the chest, with the arcading becoming tracery and the introduction of crockets. However, rectilinear tracery does not appear on chests. From the end of the thirteenth century onwards beasts appear as part of the design; then figures and saints, eventually forming whole scenes. These were usually combined with tracery and geometric designs, which were not replaced. The two developed side by side.

Framed and Panelled Chests

By the fifteenth century, stiles had narrowed into a frame, with panels between. This development can be traced through the preceding century. The early framed chests were just as elaborately carved as the stiled chests, and often difficult to distinguish, as they combine features of both types. Panelled chests are mostly early sixteenth century.

During the fifteenth and sixteenth centuries this elaborate carving became very flamboyant. These are known as **Flanders or Flemish Chests,** because they were imported from the continent, but many are the work of our own craftsmen, showing foreign influence. Two chests, **Chevington,** Suffolk and **Harty,** Kent, have jousting scenes carved on them, and are of the type known as 'jousting chests', which some people think were used in connection with the sport or even on the battlefield.

At the end of the fifteenth century, chests with an entirely new type of carving appeared. This was the **linen fold,** so called because it resembles pleated cloth; it has nothing whatsoever to do with chests for the storing of linen. This became popular between 1500 and 1550 (**Hempstead,** Norfolk).

Also during the reign of Henry VIII **cypress or cedar** chests

were made from imported wood (**Swaffham Bulbeck,** Cambs.).
This scented timber was repellent to moths, so it was used for
chests to hold church vestments and copes.

Jacobean Chests

By c. 1600 the plainness of some panelled chests was relieved
by inlaying different coloured woods. Previously, chests had
been painted, even the carved figures, and traces of paint can
still be found. These developed into the style we call Jacobean.

This style is very distinctive. It looks solid and heavy, and is
often nearly black in colour (**Bosham,** Sussex). Best of all, the
craftsmen very often dated them, 1622 at **Thursley,** Surrey.
Chip carving is reintroduced, but is inferior and in lower relief
to that which went before. Incised lines are also an important
aspect of the decoration. More important is the Renaissance
influence, which is especially obvious when the front has an
arcading of round-headed arches, which is very common and
quite typical. The decoration is mechanical and repetitive, but
not unattractive. **Croscombe,** Somerset, is very beautiful.

After this time the chests degenerated into plain panelled
chests, until they were superseded by the chest of drawers.

Finally, a few unusual chests. At **Denton,** Norfolk, the chest is
made from an oak screen and still has the painted figures of
saints on it. This was possibly made from the rood screen when
their destruction was ordered.

At **Winchester Cathedral,** on top of the side screens of the
choir, are six chests of c. 1520, recently redecorated. They are
'reliquary chests' containing the remains of the Saxon kings
Kinegils, Ethelwulf, Egbert, Eldred, and Edmund; Bishops
Stigand, Wina, and Alywn; also of William Rufus, Kenulph,
the Danish king Canute and his Norman wife, Emma. There
are only six chests for the twelve bodies because during the
Civil War they were opened and emptied out!

Thirdly, at **Newport,** Essex, the chest is a portable altar. The
lid lifts up to reveal oil paintings of saints on the inner side, and
can thus be used as a reredos. The bottom is false, concealing
the altar stone in a cavity beneath. The paintings are the oldest
British oil paintings.

COLLECTING BOXES

Collections in most churches are now made in wall safes,
but many retain their boxes. Often these are small modern
wooden ones, safeguarded with decorative ironwork, attractive
and unpretentious. Others use a hollow model of a church and
at **West Lavington,** Sussex, a music recording rewards the donor.

Alms boxes were introduced in the early Middle Ages and a few mediaeval ones remain. These are made of oak, with ironwork, and there are several from the late fifteenth and early sixteenth centuries, as at **Cawston** and **Loddon,** Norfolk. **Blythburgh,** Suffolk, is the most famous and one of the most attractive, with the sides decorated with tracery. Mediaeval boxes are basically large logs, most held in an upright position.

Several dated Elizabethan boxes remain: **Dovercourt,** Essex, 1589; **Bramford,** Suffolk, 1591; **Hargrave,** Northants., 1597. Bramford is inscribed:

Remember the poor: the Scripture doth record
What to them is given is lent unto the Lord.

A plea to remember the poor is frequently found on alms boxes.

Seventeenth century boxes are quite frequent and often dated: **Aylestone,** Leics., 1613; **Sedbergh,** Yorkshire, 1633; **Manton,** Rutland, 1637. About a dozen boxes have carved or painted beggars. Carved ones are at **Pinhoe,** Devon, 1700; **Lostwithiel,** Cornwall, 1645; **Halifax,** Yorkshire, 1689; and **Watton,** Norfolk, 1639. Money is pushed between the lips of carved faces on two sides of the box at **Tunworth,** Hampshire, and painted figures appear at **St. Teath,** Cornwall.

Of the eighteenth century ones there are many in **London,** of which St. Mary Abchurch is the best known.

Iron is used for the Tudor box, on four legs, in St. George's Chapel, **Windsor. Smardon,** Kent, has enamel used on it, but the enamelled box at **Witley,** Surrey, has been stolen.

Alms dishes and collecting shoes are very rarely displayed in churches for visitors to see.

CUPBOARDS

Aumbries

That recess, about one foot square, in the north chancel wall is an aumbry (almery). It was a vital cupboard in medieval times for storing altar vessels and books, linen, holy oils and the Chrysmatory. Many have been restored, others show the rebate for the door, others iron hinges (**Drayton,** Berkshire), and a few have their mediaeval doors left (**Rothersthorpe,** Northants.) Some have shaped heads and thus can be confused with credence shelves (**Binstead,** Sussex). Aumbries are sometimes found in south walls, or even east walls, in which case they were probably used for relics. **Langford,** Oxon., has six aumbries in two rows of three and is probably unique. **Swyncombe,** Oxon., is probably the earliest, c. 1020.

Some aumbries are detached wooden cupboards, distinguished

from chests by having one or two doors in the side instead of a lid. These are **hutches** (**Minehead,** Somerset) and some had short legs. **Louth,** Lincs., has its original good decorative iron hinges, c. 1500. Also good is **Hambleden,** Bucks., with an interesting history.

Dole Cupboards

There are a number of fifteenth and sixteenth century alms boxes in churches (**Loddon,** Norfolk; **Selby,** Yorks.). After the Dissolution, travellers and the poor could no longer obtain bread and ale at monasteries, but bread doles were increasingly given out from the parish churches, often from bequests. After purchase the bread was kept in a dole cupboard with open work for ventilation. **St. Albans Cathedral** has one of c.1620 and two of Charles II's time. **Ruislip,** Middlesex, has a richly carved one, c. 1692. Look for dates and inscriptions and details of the bequest. **Bread Shelves** were an alternative: these were just a rack of shelves without sides or doors (All Saints, **Hereford,** 1683).

Banner Cupboards

These are recesses in the wall, about 12 feet high, 18 inches wide and 1 foot deep, at the most. In them were stored the banners and crosses of mediaeval ceremonial processions. East Anglia and Northamptonshire have the most. **Barnby,** Suffolk, has the only remaining original door, which is fifteenth century and now upside down.

FONTS

Every parish church has a font, which may date from Saxon times to the present. (A good modern (1940) example is that of Sir Giles Gilbert Scott in **Liverpool Cathedral.**)

Rarely can the font be dated closely, but each architectural period had its own designs for fonts. Even this only dates them approximately as there could be a considerable time lag between changes in architecture and fonts. Some fonts cannot be assigned to a period with any certainty (**Ewhurst,** Surrey). Then there are all the exceptional cases which cannot be classified, and therefore the following notes on dating are only the basic principles. Most church guides give the accepted date of the font. *Fonts and Font Covers* by Francis Bond (pub. Henry Frowde, 1908) is by far the best book on the subject with 426 examples and many photographs.

Stone is the usual material from which fonts are made. Look for different types: Cornwall has a great variety. Purbeck marble was used in the thirteenth and fourteenth centuries, and Petworth marble in that area of south-east England. Alabaster is used in later fonts but of the rare early ones is an Elizabethan one at **Risley**, Derbyshire. Of the metal fonts, only lead is common enough to deal with; **Little Gidding**, Hunts., has the only bronze font (1626). **Potter Heigham**, Norfolk, has a rare brick font. The earliest fonts were of wood, like barrels, but it has been against church policy to accept wooden ones, so they are rare; examples are at **Ash** and **Chobham**, Surrey; **Marks Tey**, Essex; **Ashby**, Suffolk and **Hoare**, Kent.

Interesting rarities are fonts made from earlier work. Roman altars have been made into fonts at **Great Salkeld**, Cambs., **Chollerton** and **Haydon**, Northumberland. Several are made from Roman dressed stones: **Hexham**, Northumberland; **Kenchester**, Herefordshire; and **Over Denton**, Cumberland; whilst **Wroxeter**, Salop, and **West Mersea**, Essex, are made from drums of Roman columns. A few fonts have been made from Saxon crosses: **Wilne**, Derbyshire; **Dotton**, Devon; **Rothbury**, Northumberland; and **Melbury Bubb**, Dorset. The last example has the figures upside down because the wrong end was hollowed out. These fonts are later than Saxon, for no culture would do this to their art, let alone do it upside down. They are presumed to be Norman.

Lead Fonts

Lead fonts could be described as collectors' items! They are rare. Here are thirty-one, although one authority states that there are thirty-eight:

Berkshire	Childrey	Thirteenth century
Berkshire	Long Wittenham	Thirteenth century
Berkshire	Woolstone	Norman
Buckinghamshire	Penn	Unknown, pre 1628
Derbyshire	Ashover	Norman
Dorset	Wareham	Norman
Gloucestershire	Down Hatherley	Renaissance
Gloucestershire	Frampton-on-Severn	Norman
Gloucestershire	Haresfield	Fourteenth century
Gloucestershire	Lancaut*	Norman
Gloucestershire	Oxenhall	Norman
Gloucestershire	Sandhurst	Norman
Gloucestershire	Siston	Norman
Gloucestershire	Slimbridge	Renaissance
Gloucestershire	Tidenham	Norman
Hampshire	Tangley	Renaissance
Herefordshire	Ashton Ingham	dated 1689
Herefordshire	Burghill	Norman rim, remainder 1880

*Now in Lady Chapel, Gloucester Cathedral.

Kent	Brookland	Norman
Kent	Eythorne	dated 1628
Kent	Lower Halstow	Norman
Kent	Wychling	Thirteenth century
Lincolnshire	Barnetby-le-Wold	Norman
Norfolk	Brundall	Thirteenth century
Oxfordshire	Dorchester	Norman
Oxfordshire	Warborough	Thirteenth century
Surrey	Walton-on-the-Hill	Norman
Sussex	Edburton	late Norman
Sussex	Greatham House**	see below
Sussex	Parham	c. 1651
Sussex	Pyecombe	late Norman or very early thirteenth century

**The lead font on the awn in front of Greatham House is now considered to be only the lining of a font, but many disagree with this.

The six Norman fonts in Gloucestershire were all made from the same mould. **Edburton** and **Pyecombe** in Sussex also greatly resemble each other. Some say the same mould was used, others only the same artist. **Warborough** and **Long Wittenham** also have the same design but with variations. These alterations were made possible because the fonts were cast flat and later rolled and soldered into a cylinder. The only one cast whole is **Wareham,** which is also the only one not circular—it is hexagonal. Lead fonts also show the seams where they were joined: Pyecombe has one, some have two, **Walton-on-the-Hill** is the only one with three; most have four. There are also scars from where the fonts were locked—**Edburton,** Sussex, while the cover at **Haresfield** is thought to have been the original lid. There are usually four thicknesses of lead.

In appearance these lead fonts are shallow, steep-sided bowls: the shallowest is **Parham** at $8\frac{1}{2}$ inches, ranging to the deepest at **Brookland** at 16 inches. **Barnetby-le-Wold** is 32 inches in diameter, whilst **Down Hatherley** is only $18\frac{1}{2}$ inches.

The commonest decoration is an arcading round the side with figures below the arches, of which there are twelve: **Ashover** (leaden casing of stone font), **Burghill, Dorchester, Frampton-on-Severn, Lancaut, Lower Halstow** (this font was thought to be a plaster one, of the Commonwealth period, but during the First World War it split open to reveal a lead font inside), **Oxen-hall, Sandhurst, Siston, Tidenham, Wareham, and Walton-on-the-Hill.** The six Norman ones from the same mould are in this group and have twelve arcades, housing figures and scrolls alternately. However, when **Sandhurst** was rolled up only eleven arcades were included, thus bringing two scrolls together, while at **Lancaut** there are only ten arcades.

There are six other arcaded lead fonts but with different decoration to those just listed. They are at **Brookland, Edburton, Haresfield, Long Wittenham, Pyecombe and Warborough.** That at Brookland is the most interesting in the country. It is 16 inches deep and 25 inches in diameter. The decoration consists of twenty divisions. In the top of each is a sign of the zodiac beneath its name, then the name of a month, and below that a scene illustrating that month, including hawking, haymaking, mowing, reaping, threshing, wine making and a splendid two-face Janus for January. To make the number up to twenty, there is a repeat of the designs from March to October.

There are three lead fonts with figures but no arcades. **Brundall** has crucifixes in its decoration; note that the feet are nailed separately. **Childrey** has twelve bishops from the same model, but pressure on the soft lead has distorted them into seemingly different figures. **Eythorne** has eleven panels, seven of which depict nude men, and the other four, one numeral each of 1628.

Nine fonts with decoration other than figures or arcading remain: **Aston Ingham** (dated 1689, and has initials W.M. and W.R.—presumably churchwardens), **Barnetby-le-Wold, Down Hatherley** (includes symbols used by Edward VI—Tudor double roses, lozenges and flamboyant stars), **Greatham House, Parham** (Lombardic inscription repeated eight times and eight shields with the coat of arms of Andrew Peverell, who was Knight of the Shire in 1351), **Slimbridge** (dated 1664, with initials I.T. and W.S.), **Tangley** (shows two Tudor roses divided from two crowned thistles by sceptre, and three fleur-de-lys, so must date from after the union with Scotland in 1603), **Woolstone** (scratches described as a wooden church are on it, but another authority dismisses this as vivid imagination!) and lastly, **Wychling.**

The only remaining font is **Penn,** which was formerly thickly coated with whitewash. The font was not decorated when cast, but has scratched decoration including the date, 1628.

Walton-on-the-Hill (south of Epsom and not to be confused with Walton-on-Thames), is said to be the oldest, c.1150-60. **Lower Halstow** is also c.1160 An exact date cannot be given to these Norman examples, which at one time were thought to be Saxon but are not. (There is chevron moulding on the **Dorchester** one.)

Saxon Stone Fonts

At one time there were no fonts acknowledged as being Saxon. Now there are a few. These are mostly 'tub' fonts, decorated or otherwise. The plain ones are extremely difficult to discern from

Norman tubs, resulting in much controversy. Sussex has a group of these fonts (e.g. **Walberton**).

However, there can be no doubt about the four with Saxon writing on them: **Patricio**, Brecon; **Little Billing,** Northants.; **Potterne**, Wilts.; and **Bingley,** Yorkshire. These can be dated fairly closely.

Deerhurst, Gloucestershire, can be identified as Saxon by the spiral decoration on it. Presumably it is the same age as the church, therefore of c.1053. **Tangmere**, Sussex, has ridges like the joins in the original wooden barrel fonts, and is very similar to the wooden font of **Efenechtyd,** Denbighshire.

Deerhurst has a join halfway down, but at **Morwenstow,** Cornwall, this is a cable moulding, slightly pulling in the sides. This feature developed into a distinct waist, thus resembling contemporary chalices, hence the term **chalice font.** At the same time **pedestal fonts** developed, by leaving the lower half plain and extending it.

Decoration, if any, was usually geometric or foliated. Other carvings being Saxon is debatable, except for fonts made later from Saxon crosses.

Norman Stone Fonts

Norman fonts are very numerous, and the most frequently met with in some areas. They have survived because of good workmanship, because the fashions in fonts have not changed sufficiently to make them redundant, and because they were attractive enough to please succeeding generations.

They can be variously classified, but there are four bowl shapes: round, square, chalice and cup, and can be mounted or unmounted.

Earliest are the unmounted round ones—tubs (**Lewknor,** Oxon.), They are a continuation of the Saxon tubs but are usually more shapely and better ornamented. Saxon pedestal fonts developed into the Norman round mounted fonts. Norman mounted fonts are commoner than unmounted. A shaft, inverted bowl, or capital, can be the support if single, but more often a font had more than one support, usually a central shaft and four lesser corner shafts. Beasts are used as supporters in a number of cases: **Elmsley Castle,** Worcestershire, and **Castle Frome,** Herefordshire. After these, the chalice type became popular; **Chaddesley Corbett,** Worcestershire, is a magnificent example. Finally the cup type evolved. This has a small bowl on a central shaft, but the corner posts run up the side of the bowl and support the rim. These form a group in Cornwall, of which **Bodmin** is the type. These are round, whereas the majority with four corner posts and central shaft are square. Circular fonts predominate in the north: all of the forty Norman fonts in the North Riding of Yorkshire are circular. In the south, square fonts predominate: of the ninety-five Norman fonts in Devon, only fifteen are round. The inside basin can be square or round: the latter is probably most frequent.

These designs are used in subsequent periods and so the decoration has to be analysed for dating. Norman font decoration was copied from architecture. Books on this subject should

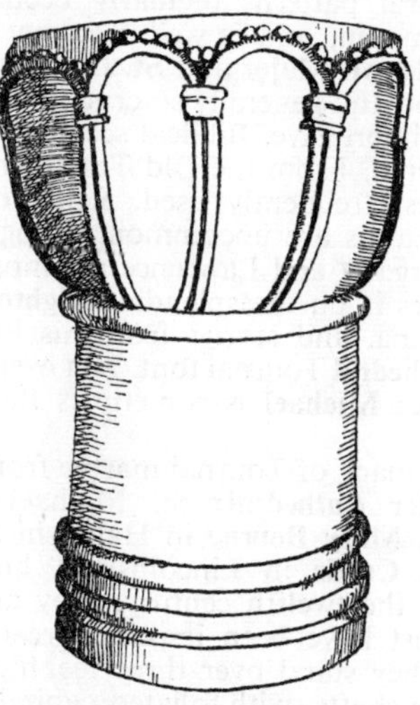

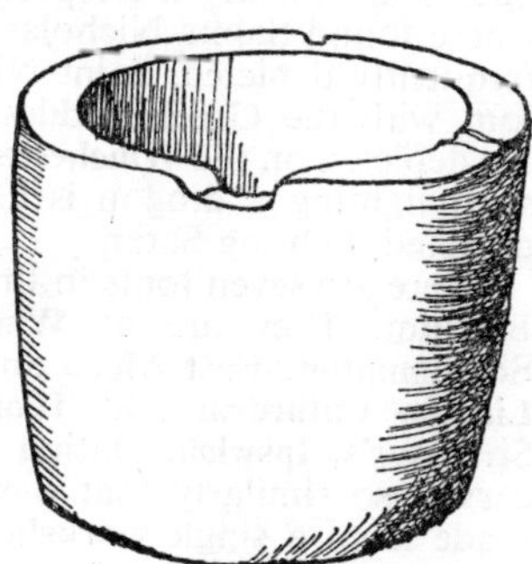

Left: Norman font with bead decoration at Binstead, Sussex.

Below: Norman tub font at Alton, Hants.

be consulted for details. A motif could not be used until the mason was familiar with it and accepted it as worthy, hence the time lag, and difficulty in dating in years. Foliage on capitals, bases and spurs is late twelfth century and afterwards.

Rings of ornament around the font are very common because they were a continuation of the Saxon culture, and the style maintains Saxon characteristics for many years, especially in foliage. Chevron is introduced (**Botley**, Hants.) and cable moulding is even more frequent. Arcading is very common, either simple (**Binstead**, Sussex) or intersecting (**Porchester**, Hants.). With arcading look for architectural details: many of the columns are grooved like those in **Durham Cathedral** and **Waltham Abbey**. Grooved columns are not earlier than the twelfth century (**Stoneleigh**, Warwickshire). With simple arcading, figures are frequently introduced as in lead fonts. Those on **Hereford Cathedral** font were defaced but many are almost perfect (**Belton**, Lines.).

Interlacings are less frequent than on Saxon fonts (**Stone, Bucks.**), but very common are strings of 'beads' (**Lewknor, Oxon.**). Instead of beads, holes were sometimes used (**Locking,** Somerset), or else very large beads, called pellets (**Crick,** Northants.). Nailhead is another very diagnostic Norman ornament (**Belton,** Lincs.) and so is herringbone (**Grinton,** Yorkshire). Frequently faces and heads, animal or human are introduced, especially at the corners (**South Wootton,** Norfolk). Medallions and diaper chip carving and floral patterns regularly occur. A roof tile pattern is just as common, and is well seen on a Glamorganshire group: **Kenvig, Llanwit Major** and **St. Donat's.**

Figure sculpture is fairly common and generally so crude as to suggest Saxon work, yet it is still impressive. Biblical scenes are preferred, especially the life of Christ. From the Old Testament the Adam and Eve story is most frequently used. Rows of figures are mostly the Apostles. Saints are uncommon, though where found Saints Nicholas, Margaret and Lawrence are most frequently depicted. Saint Nicholas is on the splendid **Brighton** font with the Greek goddess Diana, and stories from his life are depicted on the **Winchester Cathedral** Tournai font. Not every saint fighting a dragon is George: Michael is sometimes thus depicted, fighting Satan.

There are seven fonts in Britain made of Tournai marble from Belgium. They are at **Winchester Cathedral;** St. Michael's, **Southampton; East Meon** and **St. Mary Bourne** in Hampshire; **Lincoln Cathedral** and **Thornton Curtis** in Lincolnshire, and St. Peter's, **Ipswich.** Dating from the twelfth century, they are carved so similarly that they must have been imported ready made from a single workshop. They stand over three feet high on a central shaft and four corner shafts, with foliated capitals, are square with sides over three feet long, with circular basins inside. All are well carved; the lions at Lincoln are very amusing.

Another local group is of chalice fonts in Buckinghamshire, e.g. **Bledlow, Aylesbury, Little Missenden, Great Kimble** and **Weston Turville.**

Transitional Fonts

Transitional fonts combine Norman and Early English details. There are two main types: one has the square bowl with central and corner shafts. The other is new, being octagonal; it originated at the end of the Norman period and predominates from the late twelfth century. Purbeck marble fonts are frequently of this period.

Early English Fonts (thirteenth century)

Shell marble from Bethersden, Kent; Petworth, Sussex; and

Purbeck is used extensively on thirteenth century fonts. They are highly polished, rather than carved, and are all very similar, suggesting that they were mass produced near the quarries. The bowls were octagonal (**Nassington,** Northants.), or square (**Battle,** Sussex); other shapes are rare, but there evolved a beautiful cup bowl design (**Shere,** Surrey). Four corner shafts and a central pedestal are more frequent as supports. The capitals and bases were moulded the same as in architecture.

Freestone fonts are rarer and occur mostly where water-borne marble could not reach. These can be square, octagonal, hexagonal and sometimes circular (**Studham,** Bedfordshire). There are fewer pedestals, and the shafts can be detached or engaged. These could not be polished, so they were carved, but very rarely with figures (**Anstey,** Herts., has mermen). Arcading is frequent: trefoils are characteristic, either roundheaded or pointed. Plain arcading can still be roundheaded, although Gothic, so look for foliage. This is well-developed, bold, and ably described as 'stiff leaf'. On capitals foliage is less common than moulding. Nailhead ornament still appears, but dogtooth is now introduced (St. Giles, **Oxford**).

Decorated Fonts (fourteenth century)

At the end of the thirteenth century marble went out of fashion, and so did the prevailing font design: shafts and round or square bowls are rare in the Decorated period. Instead, bowls and pedestals were invariably octagonal. Unmounted fonts are much less common (**Patrington,** Yorkshire).

Decoration also changed. Arcading was rapidly superseded by niches of Early English design but with the new decorations of exuberant crockets and foliated finials. A new arch developed to the niches: the ogee. This is characteristic of the period but was never abandoned, although it lost its prevalence after c.1350 (**Howden,** Oxon.). Soon figures were introduced, although some were added in the next period. A fourteenth centu:y characteristic is a twist in the stance of the figure, called an S bend (**Burford,** Oxon.). Not all have this though. The pedestal was frequently traceried and panelled (**Rattlesden,** Suffolk), and eventually figures were introduced here too (**Hitchin,** Hertfordshire). Later fonts have crocketed gables (**Wortham,** Suffolk), and buttresses are attached (**Stannion,** Northants.). In the Midlands a style developed with corbel heads below the bowl (**Lowdham,** Nottinghamshire). **Hedon,** Yorkshire, has a round bowl, very richly decorated, yet still divided into eight panels. Look for traces of paint of this period.

Perpendicular Fonts

Fonts of this period are retrogressive, conventional and stereotyped, with much copying but of an attractive design. They are very common.

They are notable for the reintroduction of figure sculpture, which was religious, either as single figures or whole scenes. To that group belong the fonts illustrating the Seven Sacraments. There are about thirty, all in East Anglia, except **Farningham,** Kent and **Nettlecombe,** Somerset. The emblems are also shown at **Salle,** Norfolk.

Old forms of decoration are also reintroduced (e.g. cable moulding) so look for typical Perpendicular motifs: shields, emblems, Tudor roses, quarterfoils, cinquefoil heads to niches, tabernacle work and lierne vaulting in miniature, above figures. Heraldry is very common and characteristic. Pedestals were niched with figures also, and corbel angels are frequent round the bottom of the bowl (**Saxmundham,** Suffolk). Look for dated examples. Stepped platforms are extensively used, especially in the east. The faces of the steps are frequently decorated, usually with quarterfoils (**Snape,** Suffolk).

Post-Reformation Fonts

There are a few dated Elizabethan fonts (**Ellesmere,** Salop, 1569), and fewer for James I (**Whixall,** Salop, 1608) and Charles I (**Byford,** Herefordshire, 1638).

The use of fonts was forbidden during the Commonwealth, and hundreds were destroyed. Basins were used instead, such as the polygonal marble one at **Crondall,** Hampshire; many were of tin or pewter.

With the Restoration, fonts were reinstituted (**Distington,** Cumberland, 1662). Some old fonts were repaired. By this time Gothic art was dead (as shown by the uninspired imitation ones) and Renaissance design took over. **London** Wren churches are the best hunting places: St. Stephen, Walbrook. Some come from now famous potteries: Wedgewood (very rare) and Spode. Look for inscriptions and christening bowls.

FONT COVERS

Covers are often of greater interest than the font and, if modern, are frequently the finest modern woodwork in the church. East Anglia has most medieval covers, and the finest, while Yorkshire has its own but small group. In the Midlands they are rare. Covers were necessary to keep the holy water clean, and because the water was infrequently changed. They were universally necessary in the thirteenth century when it was ordered that fonts must be locked to prevent the theft of holy water for superstitious purposes. Look for the scars or remains of these locks. Look also for traces of old paint and gilding, and for inscriptions. Originally covers were made of oak, but modern covers may use alternative materials, and there are a few rare iron, copper or stone ones.

Covers can be classified into seven types:

(1) Flat lid—the commonest today and probably how they started; no pre-Reformation examples are to be found because they would provide no support for the font veil. This was a large cloth suspended from the top of the cover, hanging down all around.

(2) Pyramidal—as a dome, cone, crown of 'flying buttresses', or crown boarded over. These developed from being on a flat lid, to being on a drum, with traceried or panelled sides. Developing parallel with these during the fourteenth century were the soaring tabernacle spires, mostly found in eastern counties; in the west are more solid panels. Spire finials can be a saint, angel, dove, pelican, or crockets.

(3) Tabernacle—counter-poised for lifting. See what form the weight takes, and whether the rope goes over a roof beam, special font beam, or other device.

(4) Tabernacle—winched up for lifting. Sometimes only the mechanism remains.

(5) Immovable:
    (a) Triptych—rests on rim of font, with doors for access (frequent in the Home Counties).
    (b) rests on floor, completely covering font, with doors for access.
    (c) rests on floor, but with open tabernacle work to enable access.

(6) 'Telescopic' tabernacle spires, where the lowest stage can be raised up independently over the spire to give access.

(7) a canopy, either hung from above or from the wall.

FUNERAL HATCHMENTS

A funeral hatchment is the escutcheon of a deceased person, painted on canvas, stretched across a square or lozenge-shaped wooden frame, of sides four to five feet long.

It was hung on the front of the deceased's house, after his funeral, for six to twelve months, usually twelve. It was then moved to the inside of the church where he worshipped, where he was patron, or where he had his estates.

They mostly date from the late seventeenth and eighteenth centuries, and are still common despite Victorian restorations.

There is a good collection at **Compton Wynyates,** Warwickshire, and the collection at **Little Bookham,** Surrey, is supplied with a good explanation.

Few are particularly artistic for they were heavily painted to withstand the weather. Those at **Teversal,** Notts., have recently been restored by the girls of Queen Elizabeth's School, Mansfield. The heraldry is rarely very accurate; the silver and gold is replaced by white and yellow. The motto can be the family's but often is just sentimentally appropriate. Those on the Teversal hatchments are *MORS MIHI VITA* ("death of me in life"), *RESURGAM* ("I will arise"), *EN DEVANT DROIT* ("right is before me"). These are said to be one of the most complete sets of hatchments, and are of the Molyneux family.

The hatchment also indicates the married status of the deceased:

(a) bachelor—single arms—all black background
(b) widower—arms divided into two—all black background
(c) spinster—single lozenge-shaped arms—all black background
(d) widow—lozenge-shaped arms divided into two—all black background
(e) husband died before wife—black left side—white right side
(f) wife died before husband—white left side—black right side.

LECTERNS

Lecterns are of two types, figure and desk, and are generally made of wood or brass, but occasionally of stone.

Take figure lecterns first: the figure is usually an eagle, of which there are about twenty old wooden ones, and of the old brass ones (over forty of them) the majority are of the figure type. The wooden ones are too few and too widely scattered to indicate regional variations. Of the brass ones, there are twenty-one in Eastern England but only three in the Home Counties, and are all very much of the same design. Occasionally a pelican is used instead of the eagle, as at **East Leake,** Notts., or more recently at **Chichester Cathedral.** Even rarer is an angel; **Worth,** Sussex, has a fine modern one of 1896.

The oldest free standing type are the wooden figure lecterns, of which the eagle at **Leighton Buzzard,** Beds., is said to be the earliest. It is very early fourteenth, or possibly even thirteenth century. The eagle at **Ottery St. Mary,** Devon, is of the first half of the fourteenth century. The eagle at **Astbury,** Cheshire, is fifteenth century.

More numerous than the figure is the desk type. The earliest is at **Bury,** Hunts., from the first quarter of the fourteenth century. Of a similar date is the interesting one at **East Hendred**

Berkshire, which has one desk for when standing and another for the use of singing boys, at a lower level. Only the fourteenth century shaft remains at **Peakirk,** Northants.

The desk type became even more attractive in the fifteenth century, when the shafts were usually polygonal. Examples from this period are at **Grinton,** Yorkshire; **Scole, Ranworth** and **Shipdham,** Norfolk; **Edlesborough** and **Ivinghoe,** Bucks.; **Hawstead** and **Blythburgh,** Suffolk.

In the fifteenth, sixteenth and seventeenth centuries, brass lecterns were made. These are nearly always eagles, but there is a pelican at **Norwich,** although it is Flemish. Some desks were also made, as the mid-fifteenth century one at **Yeovil,** Somerset, or the double desk of 1670 in **Wells Cathedral.** There are no four-sided examples left, although they did exist. The fifteenth century lectern at St. John Baptist, **Croydon,** Surrey, has three lions on the base, which is quite common, and said to symbolise evil being overcome by the eagle of John Baptist carrying the word of God. The eagle in the church of St. Michael, **Southampton,** has lost his jewelled eyes. In the same church there is another old brass lectern of the fifteenth century. **Bristol** is another good city, with a seventeenth century one (1638) in St. Mary Redcliffe. An even better hunting ground are the **Oxford** colleges: Wadham's is medieval, and Merton's is fifteenth century with four lions; also with four lions is Queen's which is a rare Cromwellian one, and Magdalen's is said to be Stuart; Oriel's is seventeenth century but made of bronze; Balliol, Corpus Christi, and Exeter Colleges have old ones too. Other examples are at **Bovey Tracey** and **Wolborough,** Devon; **Wiggenhall St. Mary,** Norfolk, 1518; **Isleham,** Cambs.; **Oundle,** Northants.; **Clare,** Suffolk; **Cropredy,** Oxon.; **North Cerney** and **Chipping Camden,** Glos.

Lecterns, being movable, need a strong base to keep them balanced, especially with heavy Bibles on. A few are fixed into the floor, as at **Bury,** Hunts., but most have their own bases. These are surprisingly small in width for the work they do, and retain good proportions with the rest of the lectern. The simplest method is to have two pieces of wood making a cross, as at **East Harling,** Norfolk. Sometimes three pieces were used, radiating from a central block, as at **East Hendred,** Berks., which has strange animals carved on them, and at **Shipdham,** Norfolk, which has lions carved on them. More usually they were just chamfered. The most common method was to use a polygonal moulded block. Further decoration is sometimes added, as at **Blythburgh,** Suffolk, which is battlemented, or **Scole,** Norfolk, which has paterae. The plinth of the lectern at **Littlebury,** Essex, is decorated with quarterfoiled squares. The sides of this example are concave, as are those at **Swanscombe,** Kent. These observations apply to wooden lecterns only.

Brass lecterns have simple bases expanded out of the base of the shaft which is not possible with wooden lecterns, which thus need additional bases. The purpose of bases on brass lecterns is not so much to maintain balance, which is achieved by weight, but to keep the brass off the harmful damp floor. Therefore, the bases are not made of brass, but invariably of wood. They are usually extremely simple, just two or three pieces of wood, as described above for wooden lecterns. Lions and other features were part of the brasswork.

Shafts, both wood and brass, were designed into a base themselves above the functional base. The bases of the shafts of brass lecterns were circular with large rings of mouldings. They are very pleasing but all look so very much the same. Wooden shafts, however, were very varied. They are not usually round, but polygonal, from the square one at **Lingfield,** Surrey to the irregular octagon at **Aldbury,** Herts., with an ordinary octagon at **Scole,** Norfolk, and a hexagon at **Swanscombe,** Kent. With the medieval craftsman's enthusiasm for beautifying everything it is no surprise to find these shafts decorated. They were, however, too thin for decoration with panels, although they managed it at **Detling,** Kent. Instead the decoration was concentrated upon buttresses.

These buttresses are very varied and worth looking at individually, but there are four characteristics to look for. One, they were either carved from the solid, or, two, they were applied; thirdly, they were either on the sides, or, fourthly, on the angles. **Aldbury,** Herts., has wide buttresses carved from the solid on alternate sides. **Swanscombe,** Kent, has little butresses on every side. **Littlebury,** Essex, has applied buttresses to the angles. This last example only has an old shaft, the desk is more recent, as is the case at **Cheddar,** Somerset.

As a general rule, wide buttresses will be of the applied type, but not necessarily so. This was because it was more economic with the wood; there would be so much waste from carving wide buttresses from the solid, but less so with narrow ones. These wide ones developed into 'flying' buttresses, as at **Bury,** Hunts., which are very fine with crockets and pinnacles. This is a good example of wide buttresses being applied. It will be seen how suitable the angles between were for the inclusion of niches and figures. This was the next step, as at **Ottery St. Mary,** Devon. The example from All Saints' Pavement, **York,** goes a stage further with its canopies.

Lastly, the desk, of which there is a fine double wooden one at **Ramsey,** Hunts., of c.1450. It is said that the desks with a steep pitch were for singers, and the later ones with a lower pitch were for reading.

The craftsman applied most of his skill to carving the gable ends, like the grinning face under a large hat from All Saints' Pavement, **York**. This example has paterae on the gable edges, which are moulded as well. Another example is **Swanscombe, Kent**. The gable at **Bury**, Hunts., is crocketed. **Hawstead,** Suffolk, and **East Harling,** Norfolk, have cusped bargeboards. The next stage is to pierce the ends, which has been done in a variety of shapes, from simple trefoils, to elaborate 'rose windows', with the cusps carved. Examples are at **Blythburgh,** Suffolk and **Detling,** Kent. **Swanscombe,** Kent, has crocketed hoodmoulds.

The face of the desk was often covered with an embroidered cloth or, of course, books, and so there would seem to be no need to decorate it, and indeed there are few with any decoration there. However, there are those few with low relief carving, as at **Shipdham,** Norfolk, and **Detling** and **Swanscombe,** Kent.

The ridge was moulded or battlemented, as at **Blythburgh,** Suffolk, and St. Michael Thorn, **Norwich.** Four-sided examples had room on top for a figure of a saint.

The same principles apply to brass lectern desks, with decorations from the smith instead, such as the scrollwork at **Wells Cathedral,** incorporating candleholders and heraldry.

The lecterns, like the pulpits, were painted, and there are still traces of this to be looked for. **Ranworth,** Norfolk, has a painting of an eagle with a scroll, and a hymn tune.

Another item to look for is the chain by which Bibles were chained to the lecterns, when they were still scarce and valuable. **Meysey Hampton,** Glos., has its chains, and is dated 1622; carved on it are Tudor roses and the words 'Christian Jackets' which is probably the name of the maker or donor.

Lastly, mention must be made of the remaining rarities. Stone lecterns are amongst these. There are richly carved ones at **Norton** and **Crowle,** Worcestershire. Stone book-brackets are sometimes fitted, mostly in the chancel. There are several among the Derbyshire churches, such as **Etwall.** Wooden brackets are occasionally to be found on screens, and also on three-decker pulpits. **Mapperton,** Dorset, is said to have a unique folding iron lectern.

Early post-Reformation wooden lecterns are not very common, as most churches had a serviceable one by then. There is a Jacobean panel in the lectern at **Corhampton,** Hants.

Many churches have a recent lectern, mostly Victorian, made and presented as a memorial to someone. Two lecterns of this period which show extremes of design are at St. Mary's, **Great Warley,** Essex, by Sir William Reynolds Stevens in 1904, which is very plain, and secondly, at St. Paul's, **Brighton,** by J. Hardman and Co., c.1850, which is very ornate. A mid-period oddity is the lectern by W. Bainbridge Reynolds in St. Cuthbert's, Philbeach Gardens, **London.**

LIGHTING

Cresset Stones

Cressets are stone slabs with hollows in which a burning wick floated on fat. **Collingham,** Yorkshire, is Saxon; **Brecon Cathedral** has the most cups (30); **Lewannick,** Cornwall, has another.

Candlesticks

There are countless modern candlesticks but old ones are scarce or too valuable to have out in churches. **Hackness,** Yorkshire, has an early seventeenth century pair with foliage and flowers in white enamel on a blue enamel background. **Lutterworth,** Leicestershire, has a pair of seventeenth century gilded wood ones.

Candelabra

The oldest candelabra in an English church dates from 1460, in **Bristol Cathedral.** Exquisitely made of latten, it has twelve sconces from two globes which are separated by a figure of George and the Dragon. It is suspended from above by a figure of the Virgin and Child. Beneath is a beast's head and ring.

Seventeenth century candelabra are usually of brass, and foreign or foreign influenced, especially Flemish. In the eighteenth century they were English. The globes were usually dated (**Horsmonden,** Kent, 1703 and **Buckingham,** 1705) and bear an inscription such as the donor's or maker's name. Many came from Bristol where brass manufacture was established in 1705— early. **Wedmore,** Somerset, has three eighteenth century candelabra; **Tetbury,** Glos., has some of the same period, and there are good ones at **Cartmel,** Lancashire. The sconces of early examples are frequently more deeply curved than later. **Up Waltham,** Sussex, is still entirely lit by candelabra.

There is a pair of thirteenth century wrought iron torch bearers at **Rowlestone,** Herefordshire, unique in English churches.

Oil Lamps

These remain in some churches and range from the hideous to the very attractive; most are Victorian.

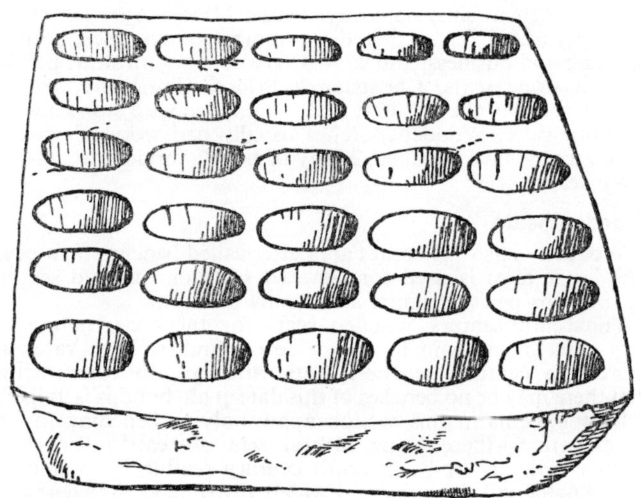

Cresset stone,
Brecon
Cathedral

NAVE SEATING

Stone Seats

All churches have seating, but this has not always been so. During early medieval services people either stood or knelt. However, there were often stone seats for the elderly and weak around the walls. Hence the expression "the weakest go to the wall". These stone seats remain in many churches (**Over,** Cambs.), more than some books would lead us to believe. There are many in Nottinghamshire.

In appearance they are low stone sills built up from the floor against the walls. Usually they are against the outer nave walls, or aisle walls, in churches which had aisles at that time (**Tunstead,** Norfolk). More unusual are those against the west wall. In the chancel they are rare because it was only used by the clergy, and therefore seats were not necessary. **Campsall** in Yorkshire has stone chancel seating. **Acton** in Cheshire has seating round the whole church. Larger churches sometimes have them around the pier bases (**Skirbeck,** Lincs.), but many bases were made wide enough to sit on anyway. In the Middle Ages the church porch was used for an incredible number of activities, both for pleasure and business, and so it is very common in stone porches to find stone seats. **Christchurch Priory**, Hampshire, has the largest porch in the country, and is equipped with stone benches on both sides. Wooden porches usually had wooden seats, of which many have perished. Many of the Victorian porches were given seats.

Wooden Seats

Wooden seats in churches are better called benches than pews. The latter term is used for elevated seats or enclosed seating, such as box pews or squire and family pews.

Thirteenth century wooden seats for the congregation are very rare and remain in only a few churches. Even rarer are fourteenth century benches. Authorities are so contradictory that there may be no benches of this date at all, but this is unlikely. (The comments in this section apply only to benching for the congregation—there being several sets of seating for clergy of this date.) Happily, fifteenth century seating is common in East Anglia and the west, and widely distributed elsewhere.

Benches

Originally the benches were raised on a low wooden platform bounded by a stout oak curb, which would warp little, and into this the bench ends were framed. Presumably the benches were raised to protect the woodwork from the damp floors. **Dunsfold,** Surrey, still has three wooden-lined 'plug holes' through the walls to act as drains when the church was washed out. They have chained wooden plugs, but the holes have now been closed with concrete to keep the rats out. This church has what are probably the oldest benches in the country (c. 1280-90) still with holes in the bench ends to take candles. **Clapton-in-Gordano,** Somerset also claims the oldest benches, but there are more likely to be very rare early fourteenth century examples. The benches at **Didling**, Sussex, have been attributed to the thirteenth century, but are more probably fifteenth century. Other claims of thirteenth century benches come from **Finedon**, Northants; **Fen Ditton,** Cambs.; **Willington**, Beds.; **Dunton Bassett** and **Gaddesby,** Leics.; **Eckington,** and **Suckley** Worcestershire. Bench-ends of this date are either shaped (**Mark**, Somerset), or chamfered (**Cannington**, Oxon.). With the medieval love of colour benches were almost certainly decorated, but I cannot remember seeing or reading of an example today.

Most of the old benches have been altered (**Dunsfold**, Surrey), especially in the nineteenth century, because they were so uncomfortable. The seats are usually about a foot wide and very thick—about 2½ inches generally but as much as 4 inches sometimes. The midland seats are thinner, to as little as 1½ inches sometimes. In the east the seats were very low and have frequently been raised, but less often was this necessary in the west and midlands where they were of a more comfortable design. Other nineteenth century 'improvements' include the removal of the floor platform, either completely or else leaving the kerb, as at **East Winch,** Norfolk. Also removed was the panelling protecting the side walls and piers against which the benches sometimes abutted. The space below the seat was originally either left open or else boarded in, and sometimes carved (**Fressingfield,** Suffolk). Returning to the nineteenth century and after, much new woodwork, especially benches, was introduced into the church. Most of it is purely functional, but **Wonersh,** Surrey, is more artistic, and at **Appledram,** Sussex, 1938, are the best benches of this date I have seen. Fine modern ecclesiastical woodwork is produced by Robert Thompson's Craftsmen Ltd. of Kilburn, Yorks. These are the 'mouse' craftsmen: their work is 'signed' with a carving of a mouse (**Kirkby Malzeard,** Yorks.).

Medieval **book ledges** are always level, while post-Reformation ledges are frequently sloped at an angle. Those of medieval date are also identified by their width—five to six inches; their thickness—same as the seat; their level—a little higher than the seat, that is about two feet off the floor.

Bench Backs

These comprise a top rail, and below it either a single long plank panel, or else vertical panelling.

East Anglia: Medieval benches in East Anglia were often without backs altogether, but few remain like that today (**Cawston,** Norfolk).

Three churches in Norfolk will serve to show the development of the back. The simplest is **East Winch** with top rail (battlemented) and single plank filling in below. **South Creake** goes a stage further with muntins dividing the panel. **St. German** has the back pierced into tracery, which has frequently been done in Norfolk.

In Suffolk the backs are less frequently pierced. Instead the tracery is moulded and carved in the solid, as were foliage and patterns too.

Midlands: In this region notice the vertical emphasis, by either boarding to the ground (**Iron Acton,** Glos.) or by linenfold and applied buttresses. To add to this effect, the backs are usually a little higher than in East Anglia.

West: In Somerset the muntins are wide and, together with the panels, are carved with tracery (**Crowcombe**) or foliage (**Broomfield**). This carving is sunken and more comfortable to sit against.

Braunton, Devon, will serve as a type for that county (and Cornwall), with traceried arcading on a carved plinth. This is possible because in the west the backs are frequently panelled to the floor.

Bench-ends

Bench-ends are of two types which developed concurrently:
(1) rectangular—mainly in the west
(2) shaped—mainly in the east.
The two types are equally common, and merge in the Midlands.
1. Rectangular: This style is not unattractive when used exclusively in a church, and when the bench-ends are in line. To reduce warping out of line, in the west, the ends were extra thick and they were framed, with perhaps just a top rail, or with styles. The bottoms, remember, were held by the kerb.

Rectangular bench-ends were plain (**Warnford,** Hants.), except in the west where they are usually carved, although there are scattered examples throughout the country. There are some recent carved ends too (**Wonersh,** Surrey). Medieval carving was commonly sunken, and was frequently tracery, as at **Stow** in Lincolnshire (noted for its bench-ends). Observe the restraint of the carvers in their work here, but midland ends are rarely flamboyant. In the west, flamboyant foliage appears on a fine Somerset group, such as the vines of **Crowcombe.** On the other fifteenth century Somerset ends rectilinear tracery frequently appears, and during the next century Renaissance influence is evident on heads and foliage.

At this time, carvings of social interest appear, of which many remain. They are fascinating, and well documented. Only misericords offer anything comparable to see. The misericord carvers achieved more in their limited situation than the bench-end carvers did with all the scope of the large end. The bench-ends illustrate a great variety of scenes of interest to the church users, and thus are frequently scenes of everyday life. The windmill scene at **Bishops Lydeard,** Somerset, is frequently illustrated (e.g. *Discovering Windmills* in this series). At **Spaxton,** Somerset, is the sixteenth century carving of a fuller, surrounded by the tools of his trade: shears, teazel holder, comb and knife. Romantic scenes include illustrations from literature, especially the stories of Reynard the Fox. He is the commonest character of humorous scenes. The type of humour portrayed is usually of an ironic type with a very pertinent meaning, not just pretty pictures. The church is frequently made fun of, with numerous foxes dressed up as members of the church and preaching.

The carvings of Devon and Cornwall are deeper. Look for trails of seaweed which were carved at the end of the fifteenth century in these counties. Notice also how south Devon often has conservative rectilinear tracery but in the north of the county there is much more freedom.

The framed ends of the Midlands are distinguished by little buttresses, which crept into Cambridgeshire and East Anglia.

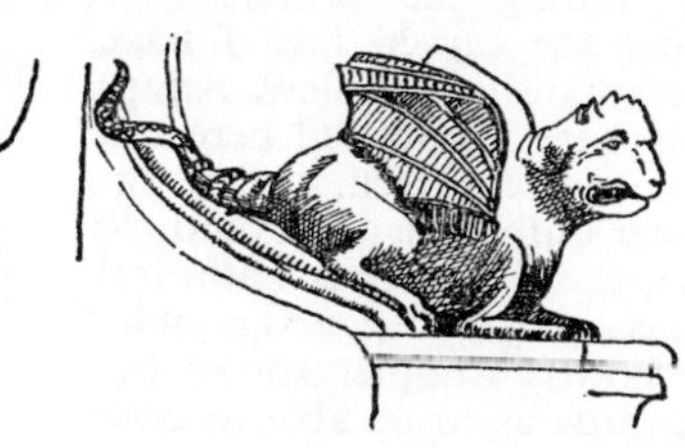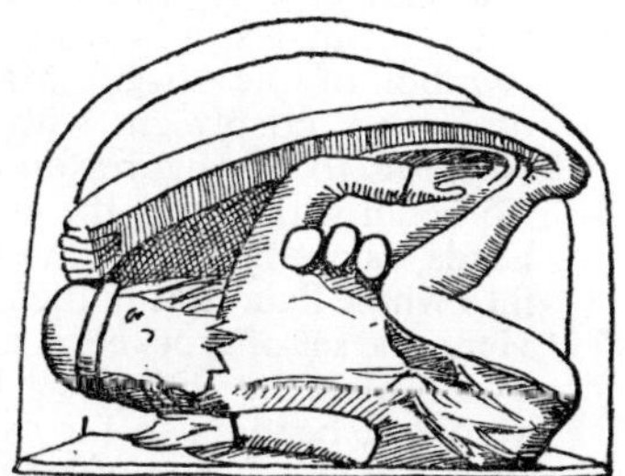

Bench ends: a dragon as 'elbow' figure in Manchester Cathedral, and a Sciapod (one-legged monster) at Dennington, Suffolk.

The late fifteenth and early sixteenth centuries brought linenfold onto the Midland ends. This decoration was, however, widely distributed (**Burton**, Sussex and **Affpuddle**, Dorset).

2. Shaped bench-ends: Shaped bench-ends differ from rectangular bench-ends by the top sweeping over two shoulders to a central higher finial. This shaping is very variable indeed, but local peculiarities are an aid in identifying ends from the same workshops. Such shaping is an attractive way of combating warping—nearly all the wood has been cut away in some cases (**Kilmersdon**, Somerset).

The finial is called a 'poppyhead' from the French word *poupee*, meaning a puppet or figurehead. The term is said to have been in use in the fourteenth century, and so originated with the first poppyheads.

It is usually bench-ends of the fifteenth century and later, that have true poppyheads. The ends at **Dunsfold**, Surrey (c. 1290) do not conform to this type. Each end is carried up and turned over into a knob, not with a poppyhead between but with a deep double cusp. Those of a later date at **Clapton-in-Gordano**, Somerset, show an in-between stage. The two knobs are larger, at different levels, more like the shoulders to come, and instead of the cusps, the middle is swept up to support the back rail. **Slindon**, Sussex, shows the final stage. The centre

31

rises above the rail and is carved into the poppyhead.

So variable are poppyheads that they are worth comparing church by church. There are three types:

(1) trefoil of central spike and a large crocket either side, usually turned down.

(2) only central spike, without crockets.

(3) finial as moulded base on which is carved an animal or figure.

The first type is commonest, with its fleur-de-lys appearance: the fleur-de-lys was very popular during the Middle Ages (symbol of the Virgin Mary). Most are carved into foliage, often very crisply cut with fine workmanship (**Ludlow**, Salop). Needless to say figures and animals were introduced here too. To begin with it was the crockets that were altered, at first into heads, as on the Dean's Stall in **Chester Cathedral,** and eventually into whole figures as in the Lady Chapel of **Winchester Cathedral.** Here one set of crockets is carved into a pair of beggars, doubled over forwards, with their begging bowls. Another shows two acrobats, bending so far over backwards as to be able to clasp their ankles. Then, of course, the central spike was changed from foliage. At **Gresford,** Denbigh, there is a beautiful female figure: her plaintive expression is nearly worn off but is still endearing. At **Blythburgh,** Suffolk, is a wonderful collection of poppyheads of the Seven Deadly Sins.

Winthorpe, Lincolnshire, has late fifteenth century seating throughout, with an extremely good collection of poppyhead benches. This church also has choir stalls, rood screen, and parclose screens to offer. When looking for poppyheads in Devon remember they are mostly on the Somerset side, the bench-ends being of the rectangular type on the Cornish side.

There is an important development of this shaped type. The shoulders would not be symmetrical; if they were, then the end would not be as wide as the seat. Therefore, to conceal and support the projecting seat, an extra piece of wood was added to that side of the bench-end. Most books refer to it as the 'elbow piece', but this is misleading, for very rarely could it be used as an elbow rest, especially as figures and animals were frequently carved on it. This type is only found in the east.

These elbow carvings show very fine workmanship. For example, the wood was cut away from between the legs of the proud looking ram at **Woolpit,** Suffolk, and how much better it is. Lions are popular in these places and so are dragons. With dragons there was scope for the imagination and some wonderful beasts resulted. In **Manchester Cathedral** there is a beautifully carved dragon, especially in the folds and scales of his wings. His face is screwed up into what is presumably meant to be a

Black basalt font by Josiah Wedgwood at Cardington, Beds., and (right) Jacobean wood-encased font, Stanford-in-the-Vale, Berks.

R. K. Lingard Guthrie

Seven Sacraments font, Cley, Norfolk.

R. K. Lingard Guthrie

Early English font, Broad-well, Oxon.

Stapled font cover at Kinwarton, Worcs., to prevent the theft of holy water.

G. N. Wright

J. C. D. Smith

The black Tournai marble font at East Meon, Hants., depicts the Expulsion of Adam and Eve from Eden.

The Norman lead font at Tidenham, Glos., is one of over thirty in the country.

J. C. D. Smith

The seventeenth century bread basket at Maids Moreton, Bucks., is a rare survival of dole distribution.

A dole cupboard at Axbridge, Somerset.

J. C. D. Smith

The 'Laudian' altar rails at Puddletown, Dorset, were erected in the seventeenth century to protect the altar.

The fourteenth century chest at Southwold, Suffolk, has a richly decorated front.

At Altarnum, Cornwall, the Jacobean communion rails stretch right across the nave and both aisles.

The sixteenth century carved wooden font cover at Swim- bridge, Devon.

J. C. D. Smith

The medieval wooden lectern at Monksilver, Somerset.

This fourteenth century misericord at Ludlow, Shropshire, shows a woman by a fire, with kettle boiling and carcasses hanging up.

The 1660 desk lectern at Wells Cathedral has candle holders.

D. Uttley

The font cover at Ufford, Suffolk, is said to be the most beautiful in the world.

J. M. Whitelaw

The medieval carved wooden pulpit at Trull, Somerset.

Late Georgian furnishings at Mildenhall in Wiltshire. Note the low settle in the front right of the picture.

Box pews, three-decker pulpit, and tester at Old Dilton,, Wiltshire.

J. C. D. Smith

Funeral hatchments in St. Mary's church, Woodbridge, Suffolk.

Medieval benches at East Lyng, Somerset, reputed to have been carved by the monks of Athelney.

J. C. D. Smith

*Pull-out servants' seats at Catcott, Somerset, and (right) an
eighteenth century poor box at Pinhoe, Devon.*

Rare banner stave cupboard at Broadwell, Oxon., and (right) a sixteenth century bench end at Abbotsham, Devon.

J. C. D. Smith

The fifteenth century chancel screen and wooden pulpit at Bovey Tracey, Devon.

Left: The medieval stone chancel screen at Compton Bassett, Wiltshire, originally came from Salisbury Cathedral.

J. C. D. Smith

Above: Medieval candelabra at Rowlestone, Herefords.

Brass chandelier presented to Frampton church, Lincs., in 1722.

fierce snarl, but to me it looks as though the creature has burst into tears! Of figures, angels are the most popular, and are usually sitting down, just as animals are frequently on their haunches. In the Lady Chapel of **Winchester Cathedral** are some striking figures—dignitaries of the church, such as the bishop and the prior in their pulpits.

Shaped bench-ends are not carved to the same extent as the rectangular ones. Many are left plain, or just chamfered (**Slindon, Sussex**). Others have simple tracery (**Wellow,** Somerset) or elaborate work (**Dennington,** Suffolk). Figures are not nearly so common as on the rectangular ends, and the thickness of the ends only permits them to be carved in low relief (Dean's Stall, **Chester Cathedral**). However, occasionally, as at **Wiggenhall St. Mary,** Norfolk, the end is thick enough to take an alcove and figure, in high relief, on a pedestal. In the type with an 'elbow' there is usually a distinction in the decoration between the bench-end proper and the additional piece. The latter is frequently treated as a buttress. (See J. C. Cox—*Bench-ends in English Churches*—1916).

Box Pews

After the Reformation, and especially during the Georgian period, benches were replaced by enclosed seating, known as box pews and satirized as 'horse boxes'. In terms of comfort they were an improvement for they shielded the legs from draughts. Many were removed during the nineteenth century, but most counties have several churches retaining these furnishings (**Idsworth,** Hants.). The finest is **Mildenhall,** Wiltshire, which has almost a complete set of furnishings of this period.

Box pews are invariably plain compared with what went before, but **Fairfield,** Kent, has six box pews painted white with black edging, and **Stokesay,** Salop, has small carved panels. About 1642 it became general for locks to be fitted, of which several interesting records remain, and of the controversy which frequently arose over them. Samuel Pepys writes in his diary of being kept waiting because the sexton had not unlocked the pew.

Box pews are usually described with three-decker pulpits which evolved at the same time. At **Fairfield** there is a small pew opening into a higher pew which serves as a reading desk and pulpit.

Private Pews

In the early Middle Ages (e.g. 1287—Synod of Exeter) the reserving of places in churches was stopped because too much time was wasted bickering over them. To overcome this, the wealthy endowed themselves with private chantries, but Henry

VIII supressed these at the Reformation, and so the wealthy had their own private pews. Usually this right was reserved for the patron of the church—the Lord of the Manor, hence the term 'Squire's Pew'. They are also called Family Pews because they were large enough to accommodate the whole family.

Most date from the seventeenth century and so are in fact box pews. **Whalley,** Lancashire, has both seventeenth and eighteenth century ones. They are much larger and more dignified than box pews, with screen work round them, and sometimes a roof. The former are termed 'open' and the latter 'canopied'. **Holcombe Rogus,** Devon, is of the open type and is ornamented with medallions on the screenwork, carved into low relief with Biblical and other scenes. This work shows the influence of the Italian Renaissance. **Tawstock,** Devon, illustrates the canopy type, in the form of a roof, and coloured.

Pew roofs became fashionable in the early seventeenth century. They were supported upon posts, somewhat similar to four poster beds, which is how Swift satirized them in *Baucus and Philemon*. Such a pew is at **Teversal,** Notts., and is still equipped with hat pegs. Most of these manorial pews are very comfortably furnished, of which the best example is **Gatton,** Surrey. This, like **Parham,** Sussex, and **Cottesbrooke,** Northants., and several others, has a fireplace! The last example is of two storeys, like one at **Rycote,** Oxon., which was used by Charles I. In the same chapel is an earlier one used by Elizabeth I. These are either side of the nave, replacing the rood screen. At St. Margaret Pattens, are two magnificent canopied pews, which are the only ones left in **London.** One is inscribed 'C.W. 1686' and is believed to be Sir Christopher Wren's, who built the present church. At the old church, **Esher,** Surrey (now a school) the south transept is a private pew, built 1725-6. **Breedon,** Leics., and **Ellingham,** Hants., also have family pews, which are not uncommon. They are usually in the nave, but since the early Middle Ages the lay rector who is often also the squire has had the right to a seat in the chancel. There are simple chancel box pews at **Up Marden,** Sussex.

A second type of private pew belongs to the local corporation. Such a pew exists at **Bridgwater,** Somerset, and the carving suggests it was made from the rood screen. The seats for the borough council at **Queenborough,** Kent, have the town arms carved and painted on the centre one. At. St. Mary Pattens, **London,** is a Beadle's Pew, and a Punishment Bench for those who misbehaved during a service. It is carved with a devil's head!

PULPITS

Every church today has a pulpit, but this was not so in the Middle Ages. Instead, the altar steps were used, and occasionally the rood screen or pulpitum. There is only one reference to pulpits in the Bible: "Ezra the scribe stood upon a pulpit of wood" (Nehemiah, ch. VIII, v. 4), and only one reference in the Holy Scriptures: the rubric introduction to the Commination Service demands that the priest says the office "in the Reading-Pew or pulpit" (English Prayer Book). There are about one hundred pre-Reformation wooden pulpits left, of which Norfolk has over twenty and Devon about fifteen. About sixty stone pulpits are medieval of which Gloucestershire has about a dozen and Devon nearly as many. Stone pulpits are largely confined to areas with good stone from which to make them.

Although known to have existed in the twelfth century, the earliest surviving examples are the stone refectory pulpits at **Chester** and **Beaulieu**, Hants. The earliest wooden one is c. 1330 (very rare) at **Fulbourne**, Cambs. Other fourteenth century pulpits are at **Upper Winchendon,** Bucks., and **Evenlode** and **Stanton** (1375), Glos.

A canon of 1603 ordered that *all* churches should possess a pulpit, hence the large number of this time, which we loosely call 'Jacobean'.

Sometimes pulpits stood against the first pier west of the chancel screen, either on the north or on the south side, but restorers loved to move them back against the screen. Today very few are in their original positions. Medieval pulpits are immediately recognizable by their beautiful tall narrow proportions, dictated by the proportions of the church they furnish. Although Post-Reformation designers rarely took this into consideration, their work is usually in sympathy with the church where it has not been subsequently altered. Their pulpits are low and bulky and so impossible to make beautiful. Many were given new stone bases of squat proportions in the nineteenth century. The three-decker pulpits of the late seventeenth and early eighteenth centuries were, however, in keeping with the high box pews of that time, though not always attractive. These high backed pews and galleries necessitated the preacher being high up, on the top deck. The reader occupied the middle deck, and the clerk the lowest. These were mostly removed during the nineteenth century, but quite a number remain (**Stanstead Abbots,** Herts.). **Mildenhall,** Wilts., retains one with all the other contemporary fittings. Another church noted more for its fittings than architecture is **Shelland,** Suffolk, which has a three-decker. The alternative to these was to elevate the ordinary pulpit. This resulted in much mutilation.

Medieval Wooden Pulpits

Square pulpits quickly developed into the more beautiful polygonal shapes. Hexagonal are commonest, then octagonal with their taller, narrower and more attractive panels. The pulpits at **Selworthy** and **Long Sutton,** Somerset, have twelve and sixteen sides respectively. Occasionally the sides are concave, **(Cockington,** Devon). Alternatively, they may be of unequal size, as at **East Hagbourne,** Berks. (fifteenth century), with narrow and wide alternating, or as at **Wendens Ambo,** Essex (fifteenth century), with seven wide and two narrow sides. A further variation is the incomplete polygon; five sides of an octagon being commonest.

The one or two doors of these old pulpits have usually gone, or been incorporated elsewhere in the church. Those from St. Anne's, **Lewes,** Sussex, are said to be in the castle. Look for the hinge marks though. Similarly, the medieval wooden steps or ladders needed have usually gone, less so the stone ones, still at St. Peter's, **Wolverhampton.** Post-Reformation examples are of course more common, e.g. the early eighteenth century ones at **Ipplepen,** Devon (the pulpit is medieval).

The construction of pulpits is varied and worth a close look. Simplest are those carved from a solid block of wood, as at **Mellor,** Derbyshire. This does not necessarily indicate an early date, for the beautiful example at **Chilverstone,** Devon, has linen-fold decoration, which dates it to the late fifteenth or early sixteenth century. The second method of construction is to have a separate slab per side. There is a fine group in Somerset, with **Queen Camel** as the type. Thirdly, the commonest method is framed, with sill, rail, angle-posts, and panels.

These angle posts were frequently extended to form legs: nine at **Wendens Ambo,** Essex, and six at St. Mary de Lode, **Gloucester.** Alternatively, the pulpit may be supported upon a block of masonry, usually octagonal: a method used at all times. Thirdly, a stem or shaft may be the support, usually hexagonal or octagonal, but in the east mostly round. These are too slender for decoration, but in the west these are stouter and so sometimes traceried. These principles also apply to the ribs of the type where the stem branches out into coving: the wine-glass type. Notice that there are no lierne ribs in the coving.

The sill is usually only moulded, and the frame generally so—emphasized in western counties, but eastern ones have minimum proportions. The obvious way to treat the corners is to carve them into buttresses, with considerable variation. Such appear on pulpits of all ages, except in Devon and Cornwall, but are most common in midland and eastern counties. Cornices are plain and small in the east but decorated in the west.

The panels received the greatest attention, with often highly intricate tracery, or more formal rectilinear tracery. Less often was it worked out of the solid, than applied, which is a characteristic of a west Somerset group of pulpits, including **Monksilver.** A niche per panel was an ideal development and most common in the west, but **Edlesborough,** Bucks., is an eastern example. The niches were hooded with canopies of various constructions but those caught back, as at **Harberton,** are found only in Devon. The destruction at the Reformation was especially fierce on these niche figures, but some remain (**Trull,** Somerset) although some niches were possibly only decorative.

Testers or sounding boards over the pulpits are mostly seventeenth century, and were large, supported upon a standard or backpiece. Many of the Jacobean ones are very pleasing in design and decoration, with shallow carving and inlay work. **Pyrford,** Surrey, dated 1628, has this attractive inlaying, and pendants as well. **South Burlingham,** Norfolk, has a Renaissance tester, and there is a fine Wren tester in St. Clement, **London.** There are only about six medieval testers: **Edlesborough,** Bucks., is the finest, with octagonal tabernacled spire and lierne vaulting.

In the fifteenth and sixteenth centuries pulpits were sometimes dated. There are believed to be only two for Edward VI: **Alfpuddle,** Dorset, 1547, and **Chedzoy,** Somerset, 1551. There are a few Elizabethan ones: **Knebworth,** Herts., 1567, and **Lenham,** Kent, 1574. (The latter church has excellent furnishings.) There are quite a number for James I, but few Carolean ones: **Boscombe,** Wilts., 1633 and **Crayke,** Yorks., 1637. A magnificent Carolean pulpit is at **Newport,** Isle of Wight.

Inscriptions can also be found, such as requests for prayers for the donors: **Rossington,** Yorks. (fifteenth century) and **Heighington,** Durham. A German or Dutch pulpit at **Worth,** Sussex, dated 1577, has a carved text in German from John: XIV: 23: *If a man love Me, he will keep my words, and my Father will love him and we will come unto him and make our abode with him.* At **Odstock,** Wilts., 1580, the inscription could be misinterpreted humorously:

> *God bless and save our royal queen,*
> *The like on earth was never seen.*

Pulpits, and especially any figures on them, were painted, even the stone ones. Coloured examples, or traces of colour are still extant, **Castle Acre,** Norfolk and **Kenton,** Devon. Alternatively, the panels themselves had the figures painted on, as at **Horsham St. Faith,** Norfolk (1480), and **Southwold,** Suffolk. During

Georgian times some pulpits were grained in imitation of the new fashionable foreign timbers like mahogany (**Sall**, Norfolk).

Of the early Renaissance pulpits, **Worth,** Sussex, has a very elaborate continental pulpit, with figures of the twelve evangelists, and applied carving. **Blythburgh,** Suffolk, has panelling and low relief carving, a widely projecting bookboard, decorated beneath, on large carved brackets. It is supported upon four legs. **Edington,** Wilts., shows more restraint and refinement.

With Jacobean pulpits there was once again regard for proportion, and most are very pleasing, with the typical round-headed arcading. Decoration otherwise is usually low relief carving, chip carving, inlay work and incised lines: **Cheddington,** Bucks., and **Caerwent,** Monmouthshire.

Somerset has some Carolean examples, sometimes with figures, like Father Time at **Stoke St. Gregory. Chaldon,** Surrey, 1657, and **Rotherfield,** Sussex, are rare Cromwellian examples. St. John's, **Leeds,** 1631, has a pulpit and tester among a fine collection of contemporary furnishings. Look for the work of Grinling Gibbons (1648-1721), especially in **London** (St. Andrew's, Holborn). There is a magnificent example of his work at **Graveney,** Kent.

Medieval Stone Pulpits

These are less ornate and usually follow the current architectural style. Mostly they are built on to or against walls and piers: **Clymping,** Sussex and **Long Coombe,** Oxon., c. 1370. **Witheridge,** Devon (late fifteenth century), is closer to wooden pulpits in style, with its traceried shaft, foliage trails and carved figures in niches in the panels. **Arundel,** Sussex, and **Cold Ashton,** Glos., are the only two with stone canopies. The former has had the colouring restored on the little vaulted roof.

Metal Pulpits

Metal pulpits of any great age have not survived in Britain, so all metal pulpits are recent. There is an ironwork one at **Hadlow Down,** Sussex, and a splendid new (1966) aluminium faced one in **Chichester Cathedral.**

There are over sixty **hour glass stands,** but less glasses remaining on pulpits.

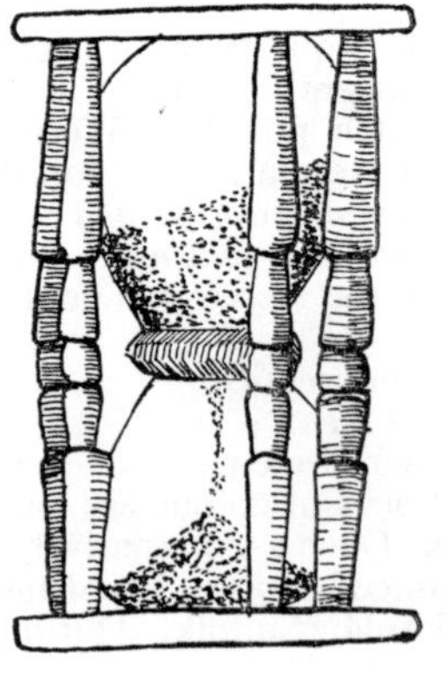

*Pulpit hour glass—
typical design*

Pre-Reformation examples *do* exist but their display on frames did not become general until the Reformation, when they were used to symbolise royal supremacy.

TUDOR arms can be recognized by having the Welsh dragon and a lion as supporters.

HENRY VIII (1509-47). Rare, because on his death they were replaced by his successor's, the boy-king Edward VI, by order of his Protector and Council. It was these arms that replaced the rood on the rood screen.

EDWARD VI (1547-53). Rare, because his successor, Queen Mary, had them torn down.

MARY (1553-58). Only one example (**Waltham Abbey,** Essex).

ELIZABETH I (1558-1603). Became general. She reintroduced their placing in conspicuous places, such as on the rood.
ARMS: 1 & 4—France—three gold fleur-de-lys on blue
2 & 3—England—three gold lions on red.
Those at **Ludham,** Norfolk, have an interesting history. Other examples are **Basingstoke** in Hampshire, 1576, and **Greens Norton,** 1592, in Northants.

STUART arms are the same as the Tudor's except the Welsh dragon is replaced by a unicorn.

JAMES I (1603-25). Uncommon. Found in Cornwall at **Blesland,** 1604; **Lanhydrock** and **South Petherwin,** and in Somerset at **Winsford,** 1609.

CHARLES I (1625-49). Rare; usually defaced, with 'Status Armys' (plain cross) painted over them. The little church at **Burton,** Sussex has these painted on the south wall—very rare. At **Abbey Dore,** Herefordshire, they surmount the entrance through Abel's screen. Examples in Cornwall are at **St. Newlyn** and **St. Mylor,** while across England, in Suffolk, they can be seen at **Mellis,** 1634, and **Ashbocking,** 1640.
ARMS: 1 & 4—England, France—three gold fleur-de-lys on blue
2—Scotland—red lion and border on gold
3—Ireland—gold harp on blue.

CHARLES II (1660-85). Became compulsory with the restoration of the monarchy; therefore, common, especially in the West.

JAMES II (1685-89). Rare; **partly due to short reign. St. Sampson,** Cornwall.

WILLIAM and MARY (1689-94), **WILLIAM III** (1694-1702).
ARMS: added gold lion on blue, in centre of Stuart arms, in
1684. **St. Breward,** Cornwall.

ANNE (1702-14). Most frequent, because popular with the
Church owing to 'Queen Anne's Bounty' (i.e. the restitution she
instigated of church endowments which had been suspended in
1534). One such church to benefit was **Porchester,** Hants., where
her arms are displayed.

A reference to Queen Anne's Bounty can be seen by the west
door at **Chepstow,** Monmouthshire. A board recalls: "Anno
Dni 1715 John Clare Esq. of Roggeston-Grange gave 100 L: to
meet ye Bounty of our late most Gracious Queen Anne for
Augementing the Vicarage of Chepstow".
ARMS: Stuart until 1707, when union with Scotland was
achieved.
1 & 4—England with Scotland.
2—three fleur-de-lys of France
3—harp of Ireland.

GEORGE I (1714-27). A popular way of showing loyalty,
and dispelling Jacobite sympathies.

GEORGE II (1727-70), **GEORGE III** (1770-1830).
ARMS: are particularly interesting because the German
heraldry was excessively complicated and therefore,
variously simplified. Until 1800, little more than the
white horse of Hanover was added in the centre, and
all German influence was ultimately abandoned.
The fleur-de-lys went out of use c. 1800.
1801-37: 1 & 4—England
2—Scotland
3—Ireland
white horse in centre.
1837—the same but without the horse.

WILLIAM IV (1830-37). Example at **Oddington,** Glos.

VICTORIA (1837-1901). Very few, and even fewer afterwards.

GEORGE V (1910-36). A very rare example is at **Trentishoe,**
Devon.

Palimpsest Arms. These are always worth looking for, and
into, and are available from all periods, but seem especially
frequent from the seventeenth century. **Lymington,** Hants.,
has been used three times. Another interesting one is at **Giggleswick,** Yorkshire. One of the seventeenth century examples is at
North Walsham, Norfolk, 1661, which is a palimpsest on top of the
Commonwealth arms.

The arms just discussed are on frames. However, they may be found in various places, but not so much as furniture as decoration, no matter how purposeful, such as on tombs. One example not on a frame, but definitely a furnishing, is at **North Marden,** Sussex. It is cast in iron, only eight inches wide, and surprisingly attractive. It is displayed over a low arch where it can be well seen.

SCREENS, LOFTS AND GRILLES

Screens are made of wood, stone, or iron, and can be classified according to the purpose they were designed for, and by the types of construction.

Chancel Screens

The chancel was the responsibility of the priest, and the nave was the responsibility of the people. To divide the two, especially for legal reasons, a screen was placed across the chancel arch: the chancel screen. This may also have been used to safeguard the High Altar and the Blessed Sacrament (hanging in a pyx above the altar) from sacrilege, but few screens had doors and fewer had locks. Whilst these screens were simple and crude the mason continued to decorate the chancel arch, but as the screens became more beautiful so the arches became simpler. Eventually screens replaced the nave/chancel wall altogether, and stretched right across the church (**Usk,** Mon.). Many churches have lost the screen that was in this position, but look for the scars where they were fitted. Wooden screens were of two designs: square framed and arched.

The square framed screens are the earliest and consist of a rectangular frame with central doorway and two side bays. A rail divides this in two, horizontally, three feet or more above the ground. The lower half is boarded in, and often ornamented with applied tracery (**Keynsham,** Som.), or decorated with painted figures, especially in East Anglia (**Eye** and **Bramfield,** Suffolk); good Victorian (1864) at **Hascombe,** Surrey. Screens were usually painted and gilded and traces of this remain, such as the delicate yellow-greens and pinks at **Llangwm Uchaf,** Monmouthshire, or else have been restored, as at the nearby church of **Usk.**

The upper half was divided vertically by 'muntins' and the divisions traceried in accordance with the current fenestration style. Sometimes the arcading was completely traceried, as at **Walsoken,** Norfolk.

The earliest chancel screen is at **Compton,** Surrey, and is dated to c. 1180. It has nine Romanesque arches and forms a safety barrier to the open upper storey of the chancel; this is unique.

The square framed type is widely distributed and commoner than the arched type, except in Devon and Somerset, and also in East Anglia, but generally in the east they are about equal. In the Midlands the arched types are few and far between.

The arched type dates from the end of the fourteenth century and is a development of the square framed, which, however, is not superseded. The new style re-used the designs of the square framed but fanned out the muntins into glorious vaulting. The climax was reached with the pendant vaults of East Anglia of which the finest is **Bramfield,** Suffolk. Note the different styles of vaulting; lierne is widely distributed, and even some fan vaulting is attempted. Vaulting was not just applied but was frequently structurally incorporated, especially in the west. Note how the emphasis in the late fifteenth century shifts from the tracery to the vaulting, but some tracery was revived in the early sixteenth century.

Stone chancel screens also occur, usually in monastic, collegiate and cathedral churches. The finest in a parish church is at **Compton Bassett,** Wiltshire, but even that came from a side chapel in **Salisbury Cathedral.** This is one of five stone chancel screens in Wiltshire: more than in any other county. In appearance they followed the contemporary architectural style, and are very much part of the fabric rather than the furniture. This is especially so where they served instead of the nave/chancel wall (**Welsh Newton,** Herefordshire). Old records often mention the replacement of a stone screen by a more beautiful wooden one, which partly accounts for the scarcity of the stone screens.

In cathedral and collegiate churches there often remains another stone screen: the **pulpitum.** This was built west of the stalls. So if the stalls were in the choir the pulpitum would act as a dividing screen between the nave and the choir, but at **Gloucester Cathedral** the pulpitum is one bay down the nave because formerly there were stalls in that bay. They too correspond in appearance with contemporary architecture, and have one central archway, and perhaps side archways also (**Chichester Cathedral**) but the sides formerly had altars. On top of the pulpitum is a gallery used by members of the clergy when officiating in parts of the medieval services. This has been revived in some places, e.g. Chichester Cathedral. The pulpitum must not be confused with the rood loft—see below.

The Rood

Prior to the Reformation the rood was the focal point of the church but they were wantonly destroyed during the reign of

Edward VI and only a small proportion were replaced in the nineteenth century (Eye, Suffolk). However, much remains for 'Discoverers' to find. The rood (a Saxon word) was a large wooden crucifix with attendant figures of St. John on the left and the Virgin on the right. The destruction of these as superstitious was complete, yet four relics have survived, including a twelfth century head and foot of Christ at **South Cerney,** Glos. Three figures are now in the National Museum of Wales, Cardiff. The position of the rood was above the chancel screen. Some hung from a **rood beam** as at **Shere,** Surrey, to act as a tympanum in the chancel arch, while others were supported from below by the rood beam, and thus were higher up. Some rood beams remain. That at **Old Shoreham,** Sussex, is probably the oldest for it is ornamented with Norman billet moulding. Some churches can show the sawn off ends of the rood beam still embedded in the wall, **(Knapton,** Norfolk), whilst even more have the stone corbels on which it rested (**Trotton,** Sussex).

The rood needed cleaning, and the light that hung before it also demanded attention, and so a loft was built below. This stretched right across the nave, and is known as the **rood loft.** (Some lofts had an altar in them, beneath the rood.) It was also used as a music gallery, with organ and musicians on it. The presence of piscinas proves that many had altars (**South Harting,** Sussex). There is confusion as to whether parts of services were delivered from them. It would seem that they were not, except at Easter: do not confuse with pulpitums. Edward VI had demanded their destruction along with the roods; Mary restored them; Elizabeth I had them destroyed again. Happily for some reason a few were not destroyed and remain today, especially in Wales. Some dioceses permitted them to remain as music galleries (**Greywell,** Hants.); others were removed to the west end.

The lofts were above the chancel screen, usually structurally connected with it, in which case the chancel screen is called a **rood screen.** Look to see if the sides are treated differently, e.g. one side vaulting, the other coving (**Astbury,** Cheshire; **Gresford,** Denbigh).

Remaining lofts are not earlier than fifteenth century, and are of three types:

(a) The earliest method was to add another beam, called the bressummer, which takes all the weight, several feet to the west of the top beam of the chancel screen. This second beam was level with the first, and the intervening space was boarded over to form the floor of the loft. This could be as little as two feet wide or as much as seven. They would have to be wide if they were to be used as music galleries as well, and to carry altars. (**Flamborough** and **Hubberholme,** Yorkshire).

(b) After the mid-fifteenth century the bressummer is built higher than the screen beam and so another beam had to be added above the screen, and the floor boarded over. This type does not take the weight on the bressummer but transfers it down onto the screen by puncheons. These floors were obviously less easily destroyed than the former method, and so frequently remain, especially in Devon, e.g. **Atherington.** Many of the Welsh ones are of this type too, such as **Llananno, Radnor** and **Llanrwst,** Denbigh).

(c) The third and most uncommon method was to build two rood screens and board the top over as the floor. (**Hexam Abbey, Manchester Cathedral** and **Edington,** Wiltshire).

Lofts with their parapets are much rarer, especially in East Anglia. The panels were usually traceried (**Llanwnog,** Montgomery; **Derwen,** Denbigh) or pierced into decorative gratings (**Bettws Newydd** and **Llangwm Uchaf,** Monmouthshire), or else solid with canopied niches for figures (**Llanrwst,** Denbigh).

Stone rood screens were sometimes built, and date from the 'Decorated' period and after. Again these must not be confused with pulpitums: rood screens were built to the west of pulpitums. They usually had two lateral doorways (**St. Albans Cathedral**) for use during the great Easter processions.

'Discoverers' still have a few things to look for concerning roods.

Look for windows added to the fenestration for the purpose of lighting the loft. There is a Decorated dormer window lighting the thirteenth century stone rood screen at **Welsh Newton** in Herefordshire.

Look also for **rood celures** which were specially decorated areas of roof or ceiling above the rood. At **Pyrford,** Surrey, only the boards across the roof rafters remain, but at **Hennock,** Devon, the beautiful bosses remain.

The rood lofts were reached either by ladders (which have perished) or by stairs, which remain. One can sometimes see where some steps have been resurfaced because of excessive wear. This is part of the evidence that the lofts were used by musicians, for the priest could never cause such wear on his own. The stairs went up the inside of the thick walls, as at **Bettws Newydd,** Monmouthshire, or in a turret bulging through the outside wall as at **Greywell,** Hampshire. The stairs at **Singleton,** Sussex, pass up inside one of the columns, and at the bottom, embedded in the masonry, are the old door hinges. Many doors remain, though usually restored. The lower doors have sometimes been converted to other uses: the entrance to the organ at St.

Mary's, **Guildford,** Surrey, and the pulpit at **Monksilver,** Somerset. The upper doors remain less often, having been frequently destroyed by the addition of aisles, especially in Victorian enlargements. Therefore many are now just holes in the wall, but some do remain. Sometimes it is the stairs that have gone, as at **South Warnborough,** Hampshire.

Rood beams from which the rood was suspended enable one to see from below where the rood was fastened. Rood beams of the second type, that support the rood from below, are very difficult to see with respect to these scars. There are said to be some which still have holes for burning tapers.

Behind the roods, either on the wall, or on boards inserted into the chancel arch as a tympanum, were appropriate paintings, such as the Doom and Last Judgment. Look for these: they are a good find. At the Reformation most were destroyed, or were painted over and replaced with suitable texts or Royal arms. At **Wonersh,** Surrey, the chancel arch bears grooves into which the tympanum fitted, while at **Burton,** Sussex, the tympanum has the Ten Commandments painted over it. At St. Michael's, **St. Albans,** Herts., there is a very interesting fragment of Doom painting, showing the dead rising from their graves at the Last Trump. It is painted on boards which acted as a tympanum while the rest of the Doom was distempered into the surrounding wall. This was destroyed in 1808 but a painting nearby shows the whole composition as it was discovered. The remaining fragment is interesting because it shows where the stem of the crucifix of the rood stood. (See *Discovering Wall Paintings* in this series.)

Lastly, many rood screens have been cut up and used elsewhere in the church. So have the lofts, but to a lesser extent. Very often they have been removed to the west end, especially if the church has a west tower and benefits from a screen dividing it from the nave. At **Compton,** Surrey, the chancel screen of c. 1620 (Jacobean) has been moved back there. It is an ornate example, but not very inspired. Remains of the rood screens and lofts are difficult to identify when cut up and used elsewhere; one example is the fifteenth century screen in St. Mary's, **Guildford,** Surrey, which some say is the rood screen, some say is a reredos, and some say is just a side screen. It now divides the south aisle from the south transept.

Parclose Screens

Parclose screens are those which are used in the body of the church to divide the little chapels from the rest of the church. These **chantry chapels** were mostly built during the medieval period by wealthy persons as memorials in which prayers were said for them after death, or as private chapels for the guilds.

(See *Medieval Chantries and Chantry Chapels* by C. H. Cook, Phoenix). The parclose screens are either made of stone, which is most uncommon but found in Suffolk at **Southwold** and **Wingfield,** or else made of wood. The wooden ones are usually square framed: the arched type is rare. **Cirencester** in Gloucestershire has some good parclose screens around the chantry chapels of the wool guilds. They are fifteenth century, but most of the original decorative work has gone. In the seventeenth century a cresting was added, and in 1906 canopies were added. At this date the plain eastern side was carved and partly decorated with gilding and paint. Also of interest are the eighteenth century coats of arms. Compare the work of the different periods on these screens. **Dennington,** Suffolk, has probably the finest and rarest side or parclose screens, for they have lofts on top, dating from about 1450. All these screens are very fine but many humble little country churches have good screens to offer. The little coastal church at **Appledram,** near Chichester, Sussex, has a very good square framed, fifteenth century screen dividing the south aisle into a chapel. Although the colouring is of doubtful age it gives a good impression of the former glory of the screen.

Post-Reformation Screens

Post-Reformation screens are usually dated and present little problem, although it is satisfying to be able to date them without looking at the inscription. This presents little trouble until the nineteenth century imitation work, which is sometimes exceptionally good. Before that the screens were invariably heavy and bold and many will think them ugly. They are square framed, showing the classical decoration from the Renaissance, although there was some Gothic revival, especially in Somerset. The most interesting of these screens are the very earliest ones showing the transition between the two styles. However it is more often on tombs than screens that this can be seen, as on the stone screen-work of the del la Warre chapel at **Boxgrove Priory,** Sussex. The more attractive of the post-Reformation screens are the Jacobean ones, but usually these are mechanical and repetitive.

Durham probably has the most post-Reformation screens, owing to a local school of carvers associated with Bishop Cosin. He was responsible for all the splendid woodwork in **Brancepeth** church where he was Rector before he became a bishop. Apart from his chancel screen (compare with remaining pieces of medieval rood screen) there are also pews, choir stalls, a pulpit and font cover of this seventeenth century period. 'Discoverers' will find much more there too. **Haughton-le-Skerne** also has fine 'Cosin' woodwork: box pews, font cover, pulpit, and lectern.

London is also a good hunting ground, because so many

churches were built at that time. This enables the woodwork to be studied in its rightful setting, but prevents comparison with other periods. Wren churches, and those where Grinling Gibbons worked, are the best places to start. Locate convenient churches using the index of artists in the two London volumes of *The Buildings of England*—Penguin Books.

Abbey Dore in Herefordshire was restored by Viscount Scudamore, who employed John Abel as woodworker, in 1634. His great screen is still there, more beautiful than most, but impressive for its grandeur rather than any beauty.

Finally, the screen at **Cholmondeley**, Cheshire, is a rare Commonwealth example, made with the rest of the chancel furniture in 1552.

A great deal of post-Reformation screen work is reduced to supports for a western gallery. **Odiham**, Hants., has two, dated 1632.

Grilles

Grilles are large screens of wrought iron work, which originally protected shrines but are now converted into gates and screens.

The oldest remaining examples are at **Winchester Cathedral** and date from c. 1100. Now fashioned into a pair of gates, dividing the south transept from the retro-choir, they were probably part of the grille protecting the shrine of St. Swithun, until Henry VIII's commissioners destroyed the latter in 1538.

There are three other twelfth century examples left: in the cathedrals of **Lincoln, Canterbury** and **Chichester**. The Lincoln grille scrolls look almost as intricate as the Winchester ones but are of a simpler design. The same design is used at Canterbury, except for a more rectangular emphasis. The simplest grille is at Chichester, which consists of quarterfoils in a square mesh. Notice that these early grilles are composite structures, assembled from many little scrolls, all held together with little iron collars. This was because the iron had to be fashioned by the smith when still red hot, which of course was not practicable with a whole grille.

Later, sheet iron was sawn and cut into pieces while still cold. The finest example of this, and of all the medieval ironwork, is at the chapel of Edward IV, **Windsor.** This magnificent replica of fifteenth century architecture (gates with side towers) was created from thousands of pieces by John Tresilian. It is not only assembled with rivets but also with carpenters' mortice and tenon joints. Other fifteenth and sixteenth century work can be seen in **Ely** cathedral in the chapels of Bishop West and Bishop Alcock.

Previous to this are the fourteenth century gates of the chapel of Henry V in **Westminster Abbey.** These too are made from sawn cold iron. The lockplates and handles are worth a close look, being excellent workmanship. Whilst in the Abbey, look at Queen Eleanor's tomb. The iron grille is the finest thirteenth century work. It is especially a fine achievement for the curved plane it follows. It is the work of Thomas de Leighton, from **Leighton Buzzard** in Bedfordshire. The church there has very similar iron work which is probably his too. Work of the sixteenth century can be seen at **Bunbury,** Cheshire (7 ft. 6 in. long by 4 ft. 2 in. high).

In the seventeenth century wood and iron were used together in screens, giving the solid effect typical of all work of that period (St. John's, Chester). This however, was not a new idea: the medieval wooded chancel screen at **Ewelme,** Oxon., has iron muntins.

It was not until the eighteenth century that the Renaissance affected the smith. This iron work is, in my opinion, the only really beautiful church furniture resulting from the Renaissance. The person responsible for this was the Frenchman, Jean Tijou, who had the support and influence of Queen Mary. He did much secular work, of which there are some fine pieces at Hampton Court Palace, Middlesex. These are worth going to see, not only so that his work can be recognised again, but also to see the Renaissance chapel in the palace, with many good furnishings. In c. 1696 Wren commissioned Tijou to do the choir screen and fittings in the new St. Paul's. Tijou's style is easily recognised once having been seen: mostly acanthus scrolls, with very little framework, yet with strong design: all very distinctive. He had great influence by publishing many of his designs, and soon craftsmen were using them throughout the country.

Another craftsmen caught in this Renaissance was William Edney of Bristol in the early eighteenth century. Despite war damage. **Bristol** can still show some very good Edney work. The chancel screen of St. Mary Redcliffe (made in 1710 and now at the west end) shows the same strong design, but with a lot of framework, and the acanthus scrolls have been very much reduced, mostly into plain scroll work. Although more conventional it is more delicate than Tijou's work. There is a very fine sword rest by Edney in the Lord Mayor's chapel, Bristol. It is the finest one known to me.

In the north Robert Bakewell was using the same principles. See the magnificent screens (1724) in All Saints, **Derby,** and elsewhere in the region. Some of the **London** Wren churches also have good iron screens.

The art reached its climax and then rapidly declined at the

end of the eighteenth century. However, at St. Augustine's, **Ramsgate**, is a very good collection of early Victorian furnishings (1847-52) including wrought iron gates to the Lady Chapel which are perhaps the best examples of that date.

STALLS

Stalls were provided not only in the choirs of the greater churches, but in some parish church chancels also. These invariably had one row only, and very rarely had the tabernacled canopies of the greater churches (All Saints, **Hereford,** is one of the exceptions). Instead they had traceried backs and cornices, or were backed against a screen with coving. Those on either side of the screen entrance, facing east, are called 'returned'. An exceptional case of stalls in the nave is the imported Flemish set at **Gatton,** Surrey.

Even the simplest stalls had arms, shaped for greatest comfort, often with terminal carvings for the hands to grasp. The backs were also shaped, semi-circular, and the seats usually tip up. Under these was a carved bracket or 'misericord' to *lean* against during the very long services. They were *not* for sitting on.

From the earliest complete set in **Winchester Cathedral** (1308-10), to the Renaissance stalls (St. Pauls, **London,** 1697) there was considerable development. However, the chief interest is the carving. There is the architectural rendering (by which they can be dated), the tabernacled canopies (**Chester Cathedral**), and the ornamentation. The latter is foliage (**Winchester**), animals and figures, or scenes of contemporary life, and is thus of great interest and frequently of amusement. Notice especially how the carvings on the arm rests fit into the stall design (e.g. the angels at **Gresford,** Denbigh). It is rare to find stalls of the early fourteenth century outside the larger churches, but they are to be seen at St. Mary's Hospital, **Chichester** (c. 1330).

Beverley, Yorkshire, has the largest set (68), the smallest is **Chichester Cathedral** (30) although parish churches had only a few, but where there are only one, two, or three, they were probably sedilia. They are made of wood, but occasionally some stone is used (e.g. the returned stalls at **Southwell)**. Many modern stalls exist from when choirboys were introduced into the chancel.

Much that was said about nave seating applies here, and the major stall sets are well documented elsewhere.

Misericords

The simplest type is a plain bracket (**Alton,** Hampshire), but most have an elaborately carved corbel supporting the bracket.

The bracket moulding runs off into two side carvings, called supporters, which are a British addition. **Gloucester Cathedral** shows the continental type, without supporters and with the moulding running round to join under the corbel. **Sherborne,** Dorset, has supporters merging into the corbel.

Carving is of every type of imagery conceivable, suggesting that the craftsmen had a free hand, hence the lack of religious scenes. Everyday life is illustrated instead: sports, mythology,

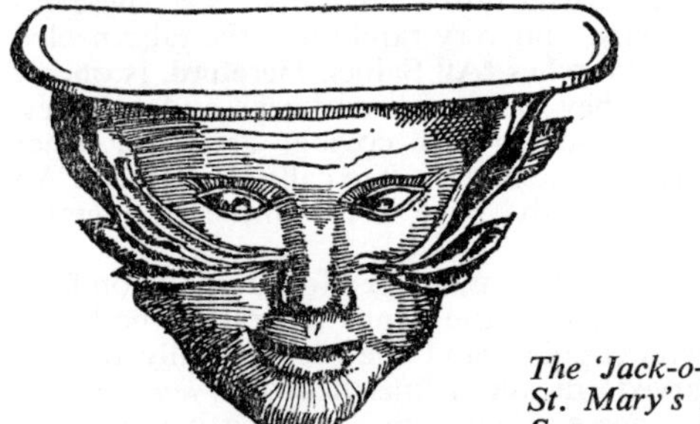

The 'Jack-o-green' misericord in St. Mary's Hospital, Chichester, Sussex.

occupations, beasts, domestic duties and scenes from literature. The degree of workmanship varies considerably, but the finest are the Merman at St. Mary's Hospital, **Chichester,** and King Alexander at **Wells.** Carvings of the fifteenth century are not often as elaborate as in the next century and simplicity returned after the Reformation. **Cartmel Priory,** Lancashire, Lincoln College, **Oxford,** and **Durham Cathedral** have seventeenth century examples.

The simple straight or curved brackets of the thirteenth and fourteenth centuries became polygonal in the next two centuries. Supporters can be separate in theme from the corbel or illustrate extra views. The latter was general in the fourteenth century, especially at Ely. Like the corbels they can be just heraldry or foliage; carved from the solid or applied. Beware, costume is not always a good guide in dating, but parochial examples are usually fourteenth or fifteenth century.

Sedilia

Sedilia are seats by the altar for the priest, deacon and sub-deacon. If a fourth is present it was for the clerk. Two or even one (**Up Waltham,** Sussex) occur.

Most are made of stone and are architectural features, being recesses into the wall, usually with ornamented arches and divided either by detached shafts or masonry divisions, sometimes pierced. The seats of some are stepped, but usually they are level. They can be dated by the architecture, ranging from the twelfth century to the Reformation. **Dunsfold,** Surrey, has a good Early English one. St. Mary de Castro, **Leicester,** has a Norman chancel one, and an Early English example in the south aisle. Piscinas are frequently incorporated in the design at the eastern end. Some window sills have been lowered and widened for a sedilia bench.

Wooden sedilia are rare, chairs being used instead. **Westminster Abbey** has a four seater (c. 1300) with a gabled, vaulted canopy. Also seating four is one at **Beverley** (c. 1340) with ogee arches and profuse crockets. Most beautiful is **St. Davids,** Pembrokeshire, with rectilinear tracery behind the three seats, vaults above, with ogee arches and crocketed pinnacles.

Chairs

The majority of churches have a chair in the sanctuary where a visiting bishop sits. These are mostly Elizabethan or Jacobean. St. Mary's, **Guildford,** has three seventeenth century chairs and **Teversal,** Nottinghamshire, has two Georgian ones. Some are dated, and the carving sometimes lends itself to 'rubbing' (ask permission first).

Among the rarities are: a Saxon stone seat, **Corhampton,** Hampshire; a Saxon 'frith' stool, **Hexham,** Northumberland; a thirteenth century seat of sanctuary, **Hilsham,** Yorkshire; a

Stalls at Warnford church, Hampshire

chair made from thirteenth century stalls, **Little Dunmow,** Essex; a fifteenth century monk's carrel, **Bishops Canning,** Wiltshire; coronation thrones, **Westminster, Canterbury** and **York,** and three medieval wooden bishops' thrones at **Exeter, Hereford** and **St. Davids,** and a stone one at **Durham.**

CLOCK JACKS

Pope Silvester II (d. 1002) is attributed with the invention of mechanical clocks, which have been in use since the twelfth century in English churches, but the earliest dials were not added until the fourteenth century, although many did not receive a dial until the seventeenth century. Instead the time was chimed on bells, struck by figures called 'clock jacks', holding hammers. The **Lullington,** Derby, clock (c. 1700) has no dial because the squire then would not have his men wasting time looking at the clock!

A few remain, not always in use, as at **Southwold** and **Blyth-burgh,** Suffolk, and **Minehead,** Somerset. Others in use are at **Wimborne,** Dorset, **Wells Cathedral,** St. Mary Steps, **Exeter** (sixteenth century) and **Rye,** Sussex (1560-2, inscribed "For our time is very shadow the passes away").

Old clock mechanisms can sometimes be seen: **Chepstow,** Monmouthshire; **Salisbury Cathedral.** There are astronomical clocks (**Wimborne,** Dorset) and twenty-four-hour clocks, hour glasses (**Compton Bassett,** Wiltshire) and scratch dials (**Elstead,** Surrey) which worked on the sundial principle, like some tower clocks (**Thursley,** Surrey).

Interior clocks occur, especially in London, which are notable for their cases. St. Leonard's, **Shoreditch,** has a case after Chippendale which is indescribably beautiful (carved royal arms at bottom).

LIBRARIES AND CHAINED BOOKS

The church of medieval England built up large and very valuable collections of books, but these were disbanded at the Reformation. After that, local centres of learning were not revived to the same scale, but many churches did again build up libraries, of which over fifty remain today.

Hereford Cathedral has the largest such library in existence, with 2,000 volumes of which 1,500 are chained to the fittings. The idea of chaining them was medieval and not post-Reformation. Manuscript books and early printed works were just as

*Napoleon
clock jack
at Wimborne
Minster, Dorset*

valuable as were books just after the Reformation. Hereford Cathedral has Anglo-Saxon Gospels of the eighth or ninth century, and in fact, 226 manuscript volumes; also, of great interest, 52 works printed prior to 1500; and the only copy of the Hereford Breviary (1270) with music.

In the same city, All Saints, has the latest church chained library (1715) of 326 books. These are on hand made chains, with swivels to prevent them tangling. Their earliest book is *Destructorium Vitiorum* by Alexander Carpenter, in 1429, and printed in Paris in 1497.

Wimborne Minster, Dorset, has another important and well known library, of 185 works in 240 volumes. It was founded in 1686 by Rev. William Stone for the free use of the citizens. Although mainly theological the books cover a great many subjects—law, classics, medicine, dictionaries, etc. There is only one manuscript book but a collection of early manuscript music.

Apart from libraries, there are a very large number of churches with one or two chained books, for in 1537, Henry VIII ordered Bibles to be placed in church for the use of the parishioners. Ten years later, Edward VI ordered an English Bible to be provided within three months, but gave twelve months to supply the Paraphrasis of Erasmus. Elizabeth I had to repeat this injunction in 1559.

Many books remain from this period (most frequently the Bible, Erasmus, Jewel, and Fox's *Book of Martyrs*), also look for lecterns and other display areas, and chains. (**Lingfield,** Surrey.) Chains were still necessary, especially when paper was rationed and books thus more valuable.

English Church Furniture by Cox and Harvey gives lists and details of these books and libraries.

PAINTINGS

Paintings, other than wall paintings, are abundant in our churches, but unfortunately, writers of guide books rarely bother with them. Consequently, hundreds of masterpieces are practically unheard of. Probably the best way to locate them is to use the county volumes of *The Buildings of England* by Professor Pevsner. Most of the important paintings are listed, and there is an index to artists, but the series is not quite complete at present.

Taking Hampshire as an example, there are over thirty notable works and dozens of lesser ones. Commonest everywhere are paintings as reredoses, especially of triptych form. The finest in Hampshire is **Selborne,** by Jan Mostaert, c. 1520. Do not be surprised by the early date: there are many Renaissance paintings in our churches. Earlier, 1512, is the triptych by Jan van Mabuse at St. Cross, **Winchester.** There are several works of the late fifteenth and early sixteenth centuries, including **Broughton, Chawton,** and **Rackbourne.**

Beware of triptyches of differing dates. The wings of that in the north chapel at **Basingstoke** date from 1649, whereas the central panel is a hundred years earlier; by Jan van Hemmessen.

As the altar is God's table, it is appropriate to depict The Last Supper, and this in fact is very common, as at **Eling,** by Marco Marziale, late fifteenth-early sixteenth century.

Christchurch Priory has two paintings by Millais: *The Widow's Mite* and *The Rich Young Ruler*, which are especially interesting as they show a Nazarene influence on the young artist. The same church has two eighteenth century paintings, of Moses and

Aaron, which also occur at **Headley** and **Freefolk.** near Laverstoke. Of the same period is the central painting of doves and cherubs in the splendid reredos at **Southwick.** Also eighteenth century is the more unusual painting at **Whitchurch,** which depicts the Ten Commandments, with illuminations round the side.

English paintings are less common, but at **Goodworth Clatforth** is a large one of c. 1800 of *Christ and the Woman taken in Adultery*.

Not all paintings are of religious scenes. Portraits are frequent, either of people connected with the church (**Mildenhall,** Wiltshire) or of religious significance, such as the portrait of St. Philip Benizi in **Portsmouth Cathedral.**

A large proportion of churches display pictures of the building at some earlier date. These are usually humble sketches but interesting if they were done before Victorian restorations. With views of the interior look for changes in furnishings, such as the removal of box pews.

Others are more important, such as the view of **St. Albans** Cathedral, painted by Cornelius Varley, 1850. It is thus prior to Scott's vast restoration. It is a watercolour painting which is much less usual.

The acceptance of modern work by the church has been slow, but Sussex has a good collection, through the efforts of Bishop Bell (1929-1958) and that tradition is continued today. **Chichester** Cathedral itself has *Noli me Tangere* by Graham Sutherland, and the *Baptism of Christ* by Hans Friebusch. The latter artist has been commissioned to do over thirty works for English churches, including **Goring-on-Sea** and **Iden,** in Sussex. At **Brede** are *The Stations of the Cross* by Sir Thomas Monnington, which are very fine and powerful. At **Midhurst** is a triptych by the well-known artist, Adrian Hill.

The most evocative modern work is probably the gallery of work by Sir Stanley Spencer, in the Sandham Memorial Chapel at **Burghclere,** Hampshire. These panels were conceived during World War I, and are well worth seeing.

BIBLIOGRAPHY

Collins Guide to English Parish Churches, John Betjeman, Collins.

Valuable introduction; useful selections, especially of London; *glossary; index of artists; up to date.

The Buildings of England, N. Pevsner, Penguin.

In county volumes; only deals with important furnishings but for those is excellent; index of artists; up to date; still being completed; *glossary.

The Observers Book of Old English Churches, Lawrence E. Jones, Warne.

Inexpensive; up to date; many examples.

Parish Church Architecture, Thelma Nye, Batsford.

Inexpensive; up to date; includes work up to 1965; *line drawings of architectural decorations I have mentioned.

English Church Woodwork, Howard and Crossley, Batsford.

1st ed. 1917; well illustrated.

English Church Furniture, Cox and Harvey, Methuen.

1907; county lists; historical information.

English Church Fittings, Furniture and Accessories, J. C. Cox, Batsford. 1923.

These old books are available through the County Library system, but check that the examples are still extant. Libraries can also give information about books on local churches; most counties have been done somewhen (e.g. County Church Series).

Libraries using the Dewey classification system have church furniture at 247, not with the other furniture books. Parish churches are at 726-54. Look also under topics e.g. silver, wrought iron, antiques.

Travel books include many churches and often give interesting histories too. Arthur Mee's *The King's England* series in county volumes deals largely with churches, including furnishings, but usually only old pieces. Despite the romantic language and vague dates, they are still best.

This is a selection of churches with interesting furnishings. The numbers that follow some names refer to the pages where more detail can be found.

BEDFORDSHIRE

BERKSHIRE

BUCKINGHAMSHIRE

CAMBRIDGESHIRE

CHESHIRE

CORNWALL

CUMBERLAND

Beckermet; Brampton; Castle Sowerby; Crosscanonby; Crosthwaite; Distington 20; Matterdale; Melmerby; Mungrisdale; Over Denton 13; Workington.

DERBYSHIRE

Alvaston; Ashover 13; Chesterfield; Crich; Dale Abbey; Derby 64; Etwall 25; Foremark; Hulland; Ilkeston; Longstone; Loscoe; Lullington 68; Mellor 52; Radburn; Risley 13; Sawley; Tideswell; Tissington; Trusley; Wilne 13; Wingerworth; Youlgreave.

DEVONSHIRE

Ashton; Atherington 60; Bovey Tracey 23; Branscombe 5; Bratton 8; Braunton 30; Bridford; Cheriton Bishop; Chilverstone 52; Christow; Cockington 52; Coldridge; Colebrooke; Cornworthy; Cruwys Morchard; Dotton 13; Exeter 67, 68; Gittisham; Haccombe; Harberton 53; Hennock 60; High Bickington; Holcombe Rogus 50; Ipplepen 52; Kenton 53; King's Nympton; Ottery St. Mary 22, 24; Parracombe; Pinhoe 11; Queen Camel 52; Salcombe Regis; Swimbridge; Tawstock 50; Torbryan; Totnes; Trentishoe 56; Witheridge 5; Wolborough 23.

DORSET

Alfpuddle 31, 53; Blandford; Bradford Abbas; Chalbury; Charlton Marshall; Horton; Kingston; Lyme Regis; Mapperton 25; Melbury Bubb 13; Milton Abbey; Portland; Sherborne 66; Trent; Wareham 13, 14; Wimborne St. Giles; Wimborne Minster 6, 68, 69, Winterborne Tomson.

DURHAM

Brancepeth 62; Darlington; Durham Cathedral 5, 17, 66, 68; Easington; Egglescliffe; Haughton-le-Skerne 62; Heighington 53; Jarrow; Lanchester; Rolser; Ryton; Sedgefield; Staindrop; Stockton; Sunderland; Towhaw.

ESSEX

Belchamp St. Paul; Brentwood (St. George); Castle Hedingham; Dovercourt 11; Epping; Finchingfield; Gosfield; Great Bardfield; Great Warley 26; Hatfield Broad Oak; Lawford; Little Dunmow 68; Littlebury 23; Marks Tey 13; Newport 10; Runwell; St. Osyth; Thaxted; Waltham Abbey 17, 54; Wanstead; Wendens Ambo 52; West Mersea 13.

GLOUCESTERSHIRE

Aston Blank; Beverston; Buckland; Chedworth; Chipping Camden 23; Cirencester 62; Cold Ashton 54; Coln St. Denys; Deerhurst 16; Didmarton; Down Ampney; Down Hatherley 13, 15; Duntisbourne Rous; Evenlode 51; Fairford; Frampton-on-Severn 13, 14;

Gloucester 52, 58, 66; Great Badminton; Great Washbourne; Hailes; Haresfield 13, 15; Iron Acton 29; Lancaut 13, 14, 15; Meysey Hampton; 25; North Cerney 23; Oddington 56; Oxenhall 13, 14; Rendcomb; Sandhurst 13, 14; Siston 13, 14; Slimbridge 13, 15; South Cerney 59; Stanton 51; Teddington; Tetbury 26; Tidenham 13, 14; Winchcombe.

HAMPSHIRE

Alton 65; Avington; Basingstoke (St. Michael) 55, 70; Beaulieu 51; Botley 17; Bramley; Broughton 70; Burghclere 71; Chawton 70; Christchurch Priory 4, 28, 70; Corhampton 4, 25, 67; Crondall 20; Dummer; East Meon 18; Ellingham 50; Freefolk 71; Greywell 59, 60; Headley 71; Idsworth 49; Lymington 56; Minstead; Odiham 63; Pamber; Porchester 17, 56; Romsey Abbey 5; St. Mary Bourne 18; Selborne 70; Silchester; Southampton 18, 23; South Warnborough 61; Southwick 71; Tadley; Tangley 13, 15; Tunworth 11; Warnford 4, 30; Whitchurch 71; Winchester Cathedral 4, 10, 18, 32, 49, 63, 65; Winchester St. Cross church 70; Wolverton; Yateley.

ISLE OF WIGHT

Carisbrooke; Newchurch; Newport 53; Shalfleet; Shorewell.

HEREFORDSHIRE

Abbey Dore 55, 63; Aston Ingham 13, 15; Aymestry; Brinsop; Brockhampton by Ross; Burghill 13, 14; Byford 20; Canon-Pyon; Castle Frome 16; Clodock; Croft; Eardisley; Hereford Cathedral 17, 68, 69; How Caple; Kenchester 13; Knill; Llandinabo; Mornington-on-Wye; Pixley; Richard's Castle; Rowlestone 26; St. Margaret's; Welsh Newton 58, 60.

HERTFORDSHIRE

Aldbury 24; Anstey 19; Baldock; Bishop's Hatfield; Bishop's Stortford; Gilston; Hertford 12; Hitchin 19; Knebworth 53; Langlebury; Much Hadham; Offley; Redbourne; St. Albans 12, 61, 71; Sandridge; Stanstead Abbots 51; Stevenage; Ware; Watford.

HUNTINGDONSHIRE

Barham; Bury 23, 24, 25; Chesterton; Godmanchester; Kimbolton; Leighton Bromswold; Little Gidding 13; Ramsey 24; Tilbrook.

KENT

Aldington; Badlesmere; Barming; Brookland 15; Canterbury 63, 68; Cliffe-at-Hoo; Deal; Detling 24, 25; Eythorne 14, 15; Farningham 20; Fairfield 49; Faversham; Fordwick; Graveney 54; Groombridge; Harty 9; Hever; Hoare 13; Horsmonden 26; Ingham; Lenham 53; Lower Halstow 14, 15; Lullingstone; Maidstone; Minster 6; Queenborough 50; Rainham; Ramsgate 65; St. Nicholas at Wade; Sandwich; Shoreham; Smardon 11; Swanscombe 24, 25; Tonge; Trottiscliffe; West Peckham; Westwell; Wingham; Wychling 14, 15.

LANCASHIRE

Astley; Cartmel 26, 66; Hoole; Huyton; Lancaster; Liverpool Cathedral 12; Lund; Manchester Cathedral 32, 60; Poulton-le-Fylde; Preston (St. Peter); Rivington; Salford; Samlesbury; Sefton; Standish; Tarleton; Warrington (Holy Trinity); Whalley 50.

LEICESTERSHIRE

Aylestone 11; Breedon 50; Coleorton; Croxton Kerrial; Dunton Bassett 28; Eastwell; Gaddesby 28; King's Norton; Leicester 67; Lubenham; Lutterworth 26; Melton Mowbray; Noseley; Orton on the Hill; Peatling Magna; Stapleford; Staunton Harold; Wistow.

LINCOLNSHIRE

Addlethorpe; Barnetby-le-Wold 15; Belton 17, 18; Boston; Brant Broughton; Cadney; Coates-by-Stow; Croft; Ewerby; Folkingham; Haltham-on-Bain; Heckington; Keddington; Lincoln Cathedral 18, 63; Long Sutton; Louth 12; North Somercotes; Osbournby; Panton; Ropsley; Saltfleetby; Silk Willoughby; Skirbeck 28; Stow 30; Theddlethorpe; Thornton Curtis 18; Thorpe St. Peter; Winthorpe 32.

LONDON

All Hallows by the Tower; All Saints, Tooting Graveney; All Saints, Wandsworth; The Annunciation, Marble Arch; St. Andrew, Holborn 54; St. Andrew Under Shaft; St. Benet, Paul's Wharf; St. Clement 53; St. Cuthbert's Philbeach Gardens 26; St. Cyprian, Clarence Gate; St. Helen, Bishopsgate; St. James Garlick Hythe; St. James, Piccadilly; St. Leonard's, Shoreditch 68; St. Magnus-the-Martyr 5; St. Mary Abchurch 5, 11; St. Mary-at-Hill; St. Margaret Pattens 50; St. Michael, Cornhill; St. Paul's Cathedral 65; St. Peter, Cornhill; St. Stephen, Walbrook 20; Westminster Abbey 64, 67, 68.

MIDDLESEX

Cowley; Littleton; Northolt; Ruislip 12; Twickenham; Whitchurch.

MONMOUTHSHIRE

Abergavenny; Bettws Newydd 60; Caerwent 54; Chepstow 27, 56; Cwmcarvon; Cwmyoy; Ebbw Vale; Goytrey; Llanarth; Llangattock-lingoed; Llangibby; Llangwm Uchaf 57, 60; Llantilio Crossenny; Llantrissent; Oldcastle; Penalt; Skenfrith; Trelleck; Trostrey; Usk 57.

NORFOLK

Ashwellthorpe; Attleborough; Barton Turf; Blakeney; Brundall1 4, 15; Burnham Norton; Castle Acre 53; Cawston 11, 29; Denton 10; East Dereham; East Harling 23, 24; East Winch 29; Elsing; Gooderstone; Great Yarmouth; Hempstead 9; Horsham St. Faith 53; Ketteringham; Knapton 59; Litcham; Little Walsingham; Loddon 11, 12;

Ludham 55; Potter Heigham 13; Ranworth 23, 25; North Walsham 56;
Norwich 23 25; Salle 20, 54; St. German 29; Scole 23, 24; Shipdham
23, 24; South Burlingham 53; South Creake 29; South Wootton 18;
Thurning; Tibenham; Tunstead 27; Upper Sheringham; Walpole
(St. Peter); Walsoken 57; Watton 11; Wellingham; Wiggenhall St.
Mary 23, 49.

NORTHAMPTONSHIRE

Ashby St. Ledger; Church Brampton 7; Cottesbrooke 50; Crick 18;
Croughton; Easton Neston; Finedon 28; Fotheringham; Greens
Norton 55; Gretton; Hargrave 11; Higham Ferrers; Little Billing 16;
Marston Trussell 6; Nassington 19; Oundl﹀ 23; Passenham; Peakirk
23; Rothersthorpe 11; Stannion 19; Stoke Doyle; Tichmarsh;
Warmington.

NORTHUMBERLAND

Bothal; Chillingham; Chollerton 13; Haltwhistle; Haydon 13;
Hexham 13, 60, 67; Newcastle (St. John Baptist); Rothbury 13;
Warkworth; Woodhorn.

NOTTINGHAMSHIRE

Balderton; Blyth; East Leake 22; East Markham; Egmanton; Holme;
Langar 5; Lowdham 19, Newark; Sneinton (Nottingham); Papple-
wick; Southwell 65; Strelley; Teversal 22, 50, 67; Wysall.

OXFORDSHIRE

Burford 19; Cannington 28; Chiselhampton; Church Handborough;
Cropredy 23; Dorchester 14, 15; Enstone 5; Ewelme 64; Howden 19;
Idbury; Kidlington; Kingham; Langford 11; Lewknor 16, 18; Long
Coombe 54; Marston; Minster Lovell 5; Oddington; Oxford (churches)
19; Oxford (college chapels) 23, 66; Rousham; Rycote 50; Shilton;
Somerton 5; Swyncombe 11; Warborough 15; Wheatfield; Yarnton.

RUTLAND

Brooke; Hambleton; Lyddington; Manton 11; North Luffenham;
Teigh; Tixover; Whissendine.

SHROPSHIRE

Adderley; Clun 5; Ellesmere 20; Halston; Heath Chapel; Hopton
Cangeford; Hughley; Leebotwood; Longnor; Ludlow 5, 32; Lydbury
North; Onibury; Pitchforth; St. Martin's; Stokesay 49; Tong; Whixall
20; Wroxeter 13.

SOMERSET & BRISTOL

Babington; Backwell; Bagborough; Banwell; Bishops Lydeard 30;
Bridgwater 50; Bristol 5, 23, 26, 64; Broomfield 30; Brympton D'Every;
Charterhouse-on-Mendip; Cheddar 24; Chedzoy 53; Clapton-in-

SOMERSET & BRISTOL—continued

Gordano 28, 31; Compton Martin; Croscombe 10; Crowcombe 30; Dunster; East Brent; Glastonbury; High Ham; Keynsham 57; Kilmersdon 31; Locking 17; Long Sutton 52; Mark 28; Middlezoy; Milborne Port; Minehead 12, 68; Monksilver 53, 61; Nettlecombe 20; North Petherton; Pawlett; Pitton; Selworthy 52; Spaxton 30; Stoke St. Gregory 54; Trull 52; Wedmore 26; Wellow 32, 49; Wells Cathedral 23, 25, 66, 68; Wells (St. Cuthbert); Winsford 55; Wyke Champflower; Yeovil 23.

STAFFORDSHIRE

Alrewas; Baswick; Blithfield; Blore; Blymhill; Broughton; Checkley; Clifton Campville; Denstone; Enville; Lapley; Mavesyn Ridware; Penkridge; Rushton; Tamworth; Wolverhampton 52.

SUFFOLK

Ashbocking 55; Ashby 13; Barking; Barnby 12; Blyford 4; Blythburgh 11, 23, 25, 32, 54, 68; Boxted; Bramfield 57, 58; Bramford 11; Bredfield; Brent Eleigh; Cavendish; Chevington 9; Clare 23; Cratfield; Dennington 49; 62; Earl Stonham; Eye 57, 59; Framlingham; Framsden; Fressingfield 29; Hadleigh; Hawkedon; Hawstead 23, 25; Ipswich 18; Ixworth Thorpe; Kedington ; Langham; Lavenham; Mellis 55; Metfield; Norton; Preston; Rattlesden 19; Rushbrooke; Saxmundham 20; Shelland 51; Snape 20; Southwold 53, 62, 68; Stoke-by-Clare; Stowlangtoft; Sudbury; Tannington; Thurlow Magna; Ufford; Wenhoxton; Wilby; Wingfield 62; Withersdale; Woolpit 32; Worlingworth; Wortham 19; Wyverstone.

SURREY

Ash 13; Beddington; Busbridge; Chaldon 53; Chipstead; Chobham 13, Compton 57, 61; Coulsdon; Croydon 23; Dunsfold 4, 28, 31, 67; Egham; Elstead 27; Esher 50; Ewhurst 5, 12; Gatton 50, 65; Godalming; Graffham; Guildford 66, 67; Hascombe 57; Lingfield 24, 70; Little Bookham 22; Morden; Pyrford 53, 60; Shere 19, 56, 59; Stoke D'Abernon 9; Thursley 10, 68; Walton-on-the-Hill 14, 15; Witley 11; Wonersh 29, 30, 61; Worplesdon.

SUSSEX

Appledram 29, 62; Ardingley; Arundel 54; Ashburnham; Battle 19; Bignor; Binstead 11, 17; Bosham 4, 10; Boxgrove Priory 62; Brighton 15, 18, 26; Broadwater; Burton 31, 55, 61; Chichester Cathedral 4, 22, 54, 58, 63, 65, 66; Clymping 8, 9, 54; Didling 28; Eastbourne (St. Mary); East Dean (East Sussex); Edburton 15; Etchingham; Greatham; Hadlow Down 54; Hamsey; Lewes 52; Littlehampton; North Marden 57; Old Shoreham 59; Ovingdean; Parham 14, 15, 50; Penshurst; Petworth; Playden; Pyecombe 15; Rotherfield 54; Rye 68; Shermanbury; Singleton 60; Slindon 31, 49; South Harting 59; Stedham 9; Sutton; Tangmere 16; Ticehurst; Trotton 59; Up Marsden 50; Up Waltham 26, 66; Walberton 16; West Grinstead 6; Westham; West Lavington 10; Winchelsea; Wisborough Green 4; Worth 22, 53, 54.

WARWICKSHIRE

Astley; Aston Cantlow; Bickenhill 7; Castle Bromwich; Compton Wynyates 22; Idlicote; Knowle; Loxley; Snitterfield; Southam; Stoneleigh 17; Sutton Coldfield; Wormleighton.

WESTMORLAND

Appleby; Bolton; Brough; Brougham (St. Ninian's and also St. Wilfred's); Kirkby Lonsdale; Kirkby Thore; Ravenstonedale; Witherslack.

WILTSHIRE

Alton Barnes; Avebury; Bishops Canning 68; Boscombe 53; Brinkworth; Compton Bassett 58, 68; Cricklade; Crudwell; Durnford; Edington 54; 60; Farley; Fisherton Delamere; Fugglestone; Little Somerford; Lydiard Tregoze; Mere; Mildenhall 49, 51, 71; Oaksey; Odstock 53; Potterne 16; Salisbury Cathedral 58, 68; Westwood; Winterbourne Bassett; Yatton Keynell.

WORCESTERSHIRE

Besford; Broadway; Chaddesley Corbett 16; Cleeve Prior 6; Crowle 25; Dodford; Eckington 6, 28; Elmsley Castle 16; Great Witley; Malvern; Norton 25; Ombersley; Ribberford; Ripple; Shelsley Wash Strensham; Suckley 28; Warndon; Wickhamford; Worcester (St. Swithin).

YORKSHIRE—EAST RIDING

Bempton; Beverley 65, 67; Boynton; Dalton Holme; Eastrington; Flamborough 60; Goodmanham; Harpham; Hedon 19; Hemingborough; Holme-upon-Spaldingmoor; Howden; Keyingham; Kingston-upon-Hull (Holy Trinity); Kirk Ella; Langtoft; Ottringham; Patrington 19; Pocklington; Reighton 8; Sewerby; Speeton; Swine; Welwick; Wintringham.

YORKSHIRE—NORTH RIDING

Bowes; Brandsby; Crayke 53; Downholme; Ellerburne; Grinton 18, 23; Hackness 26; Helmsley; Hutton Rudby; Kirby Sigston; Kirkleatham; Lythe; Over Silton; Pickering; Richmond; Sutton-on-Forest; Wensley; Whitby (St. Mary).

YORKSHIRE—WEST RIDING

Aldborough; Aldfield; Bilton-in-Ainstey; Bingley 16; Bolton Percy; Braithwell; Campsall 27; Cantley; Collingham 26; Fishlake; Giggleswick 56; Great Mitton; Halifax 11; Hatfield 7; High Melton; Hooton Pagnell; Hubberholme 60; Kirkby Malzeard 29; Laughton-en-le-Morthen; Leeds 54; Rossington 53; Rotherham; Saxton; Sedbergh 11; Selby 12; Treeton; Woolley; Wragby, York (All Saint's Pavement) 24, 25; York Minster 68.

WALES

ANGLESEY
Beaumaris; Penmynydd; Llaneilian.

BRECONSHIRE
Brecon Cathedral 26; Patricio 16; Patrishow.

DENBIGHSHIRE
Derwen 60; Efenechtyd 16; Gresford 32, 59, 65; Llanrwst 60.

GLAMORGANSHIRE
Cardiff, St. John Baptist; Kenvig 18; Llandaff Cathedral; Llanwit Major 18; St. Donats 18.

MONTGOMERYSHIRE
Llanwnog 60.

PEMBROKESHIRE
St. David's Cathedral 68.

RADNORSHIRE
Llannano 60.

Thirteenth century chest chip-carving rounded